HEADING WEST

Heading West

Life with the Pioneers

— ✦✦ — 21 ACTIVITIES — ✦✦ —

Pat McCarthy

CHICAGO REVIEW PRESS

Library of Congress Cataloging-in-Publication Data

McCarthy, Pat, 1940–

Heading West : life with the pioneers ; 21 activities / Pat McCarthy.

p. cm.

Includes bibliographical references and index.

ISBN 978-1-55652-809-5

1. Frontier and pioneer life—West (U.S.)—Juvenile literature. 2. West (U.S.)—History—19th century—Juvenile literature. 3. Pioneers—West (U.S.)—History—19th century—Juvenile literature. 4. Handicraft—Juvenile literature. 5. Cookery—Juvenile literature. 6. Games—Juvenile literature. I. Title.

F596.M378 2009

978'.02—dc22

2009015851

Cover design: Joan Sommers Design

Cover photographs: center image © Hofmeester; surrounding images from Library of Congress, clockwise from top, LC-USZ62-131119, LC-USZ62-101262, LC-USZ62-133214, LC-DIG-nclc-00098

Interior design: Sarah Olson

Illustrations: Laura D'Argo

Maps: Chris Erichsen

© 2009 by Pat McCarthy

All rights reserved

Published by Chicago Review Press, Incorporated

814 North Franklin Street

Chicago, Illinois 60610

ISBN 978-1-55652-809-5

Printed in the United States of America

5 4 3 2 1

To all my wonderful friends in the Focus Photo Club of Dayton, Ohio.
They are helpful and supportive of all my writing and photography efforts.

❧ Contents ❧

Acknowledgments

I want to thank Darke County Parks and its director, Roger Van Frank, and Garst Museum in Greenville, Ohio, and its director, Penny Perry, for allowing me to photograph artifacts on their premises. Thanks to Margery Pepiot and Karen Burkett for posing for me in pioneer dress. Thanks, too, to Laura James for allowing me to use one of her photos. I also thank Brandon Marie Miller for introducing me to Chicago Review Press, and Mary Kay Carson and Tom Uhlman for advice on doing the book. And last but not least, thanks to Jerome Pohlen, my editor, who patiently answered all my questions and was supportive throughout the process of putting together this book.

❧ Time Line ❧

1754–63	French and Indian War
1775	Daniel Boone blazes the Wilderness Road to Kentucky
1787	Northwest Ordinance creates the Northwest Territory
1803	United States buys Louisiana Territory from France
1804–06	Lewis and Clark Expedition explores the Louisiana Territory
1805–07	Zebulon Pike explores the Rocky Mountains and finds Pikes Peak
1807	John Colter discovers geysers in what is now Yellowstone National Park
1811	John Jacob Astor builds a fur trading post in Oregon
1820	Stephen Long leads an expedition across the Rocky Mountains
1821	William Becknell leads an expedition to Santa Fe, blazing a new trail the following year
1824	Jim Bridger is possibly the first European man to see the Great Salt Lake
1836	Narcissa Whitman and Eliza Spalding are the first women of European ancestry to cross the Rocky Mountains
	Marcus and Narcissa Whitman establish a Methodist mission in Oregon Country

Introduction
Itchy Feet and Moving West

One of Laura Ingalls's earliest memories was of riding in a covered wagon. That's fitting, because Laura spent a lot of her early life doing that. Her Pa, Charles Ingalls, was always dreaming of moving west. His wife, Caroline, said he had an "itchy foot." And one of Laura's uncles said, "Give [him] a covered wagon, and [he's] ready to go!"

Laura didn't even remember her first trip by covered wagon. The family had left their little house in the big woods near Pepin, Wisconsin, and moved west to Indian Territory in Kansas. But they didn't actually plan to go to Indian Territory. They planned to homestead on land the government was giving away free to farmers. Yet somehow they ended up on the Osage Indian Reserve. If Pa had filed a claim on the land, he would have known, but there was so much land, and he was in a hurry to build a cabin.

The first covered wagon trip that Laura remembered was the trip back to Wisconsin. After being gone three years, Pa got a letter from the man who had bought their house in the big woods. He wanted to go west and asked Pa to take back the land and the cabin.

Pa and Ma decided to return. It took them several weeks to get back to the big woods. Laura, 4, and Mary, 6, sat on the bedding and blankets in the back of the wagon and looked out over the backboard at the wagon tracks behind. Ma rode up front with Pa, holding baby Carrie in her arms.

The road stretched through the Kansas prairies to the hills of Missouri, then on through Iowa. The little horses, Pet and Patty, pulled the wagon. Jack, the brindle bulldog, trotted along beside them.

It often rained on that spring trip. When the thunderclouds rolled in the sky, Pa stopped. He pulled the canvas top over the wagon and tied it down. He lowered a flap of canvas over the back and secured it. Ma and baby Carrie would come back and sit on the bedding with the little girls. It was cozy and dry in the wagon as long as they didn't touch the canvas. Poor Pa pulled his hat down over his eyes and kept on driving through the storm.

In one place in Missouri, a stream they needed to cross was flooded. Water swirled around, and branches of trees went sailing by. Pa found the ford, where other wagons had crossed. He decided to try, and led the team into the foaming water. The wagon shuddered, and then, as they got deeper, it began to float. Ma drove, and Pa waded across. The water was so deep, Laura could only see his head bobbing up and down. But they made it safely across.

Pa decided Pet and Patty were too small to pull the loaded wagon over the hills of Missouri, so he traded them for a team of bigger horses. Laura cried when they had to leave the familiar little horses.

When Laura thought back on that trip, she remembered the spring flowers among the green leaves in the forest. She remembered the creaking of the wagon wheels, the snorting of the horses, and Pa's soft voice singing. She remembered the smell of the damp earth and the meadow warm in the sun.

Laura was to use these memories much later to write a series of books that children still love today—the *Little House* books. Like Pa, Laura was a true pioneer with an itchy foot. She wanted children to understand what pioneer life was like.

Laura was 65 years old before her first book, *Little House in the Big Woods*, was published. She had planned to write one book, but children loved the book and begged her to write more. That's how the series of *Little House* books was born.

Thousands of other pioneers had stories similar to Laura's. Although they faced the same problems, each person had his or her own way of reacting. All these different personalities and stories made the settlement of the West an interesting saga.

1

Exploring the West

Bouncing along a bumpy trail in a covered wagon. Fording a dangerous, rain-swollen stream. Being attacked by hostile Indians. Living in a cozy log cabin in the woods. These were all part of the pioneer experience, but there was so much more.

Many people think all pioneers lived in the 1800s, when many settlers moved west. But the Westward Movement actually began in the 1700s when settlers from Europe started moving west across the Appalachian Mountains. This was when the states were still colonies. They moved into the western parts of New York, Pennsylvania, North Carolina, and what is now West Virginia. Yet before anyone could settle even farther west, people had to explore the region and blaze the trails.

French and Indian War: 1754-63

By the middle of the 1700s, most of the land in North America was claimed by France or England. Spain owned Florida, and both the French and the British claimed the land west of the Appalachian Mountains. When the British started moving into the Ohio Country, the French were upset. Leaders of the two countries met in Paris in 1750 to discuss the problem, but came to no agreement.

The colonies asked permission to raise armies and money in order to protect themselves. King George II refused, and the British officers in the colonies didn't want help from the colonists.

In 1752, Marquis Duquesne (pronounced Du-KANE) became governor general of the land claimed by the French in North America. He was ordered to drive all the British out of the Ohio Valley. In 1753 his soldiers built two forts in western Pennsylvania. This worried the British, including Lt. Governor Dinwiddie of Virginia. Dinwiddie sent a young officer named George Washington with a message demanding the French leave the area. They refused.

To defend the area from the French, the next year the British began building their own fort, where the Alleghany and Monongahela Rivers meet to form the Ohio River. This is where Pittsburgh stands today. They called it Fort Prince George. But before they could finish, the French attacked and captured it. They changed its name to Fort Duquesne.

George Washington had orders to retake the fort, but he knew it was too strong. Instead, he built another fort nearby, Fort Necessity. On July 3, 1754, the French attacked Fort Necessity and captured it. This was the first battle of the French and Indian War.

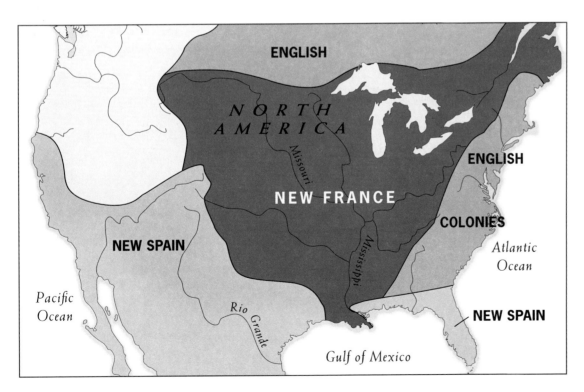

Early claims in North America, 1750.

Many Indian tribes in the area also wanted the British settlers out, so they supported the French. Meanwhile, the British sent General Edward Braddock to lead their forces in the colonies. On his way to attack Fort Duquesne, his army was ambushed by the French and their Indian allies and nearly wiped out. Braddock himself was killed.

War was not formally declared until 1756, although by then the fighting had been going on for two years. The French had the upper hand the first few years. In New York, they defeated the British at Fort Oswego and Fort Ticonderoga. They attacked another New York fort, Fort William Henry, and defeated the British there as well. As the British left the fort, many were killed or captured by the Indians.

In 1757 William Pitt, the British prime minister, sent more troops to the colonies. With the help of the colonists, they captured Fort Duquesne in 1758. That same year, the British made peace with many of the Indians. When their Indian allies pulled out, the French forces were severely weakened. In 1759, the British took Fort Niagara.

In 1759 they attacked the French stronghold of Quebec. It was under siege from June 27 until September 18, when the French finally surrendered. Now the British controlled most of North America. When they captured France's remaining forts at Montreal and Detroit in 1760, the war was over.

France and England had also been fighting a war in Europe at the same time. There it was called the Seven Years War. In 1763 the two countries signed the Treaty of Paris, which settled both wars. The British received all the land in North America east of the Mississippi, except for New Orleans. France turned over New Orleans and lands west of the Mississippi to Spain, in exchange for Spain ceding Florida to the British.

After the French and Indian War ended in 1763, King George III forbade the English to settle west of the Appalachians. A few people ignored the ruling and settled there anyway. Treaties were eventually signed with the Native Americans in 1768, and the next year that land was opened to settlement. Two roads had been built by that time. Settlers poured into western Pennsylvania.

In 1775, Daniel Boone blazed the Wilderness Road, which followed old Indian trails through the Cumberland Gap into Kentucky. Boone soon led a group of settlers west. They founded Boonesborough on the banks of the Kentucky River.

George Washington
Dover Publishing, Inc.

Indians fought with the French to defeat General Braddock's troops.
Library of Congress
LC-USZ62-1473

3

DANIEL BOONE, 1734–1820

Daniel Boone grew up in Pennsylvania, the middle child of 11 children. As a child, he hated being cooped up inside. He loved to explore the woods and fields. He spent a lot of time with the Delaware Indians who came to trade. They taught him to track animals, build shelters, and cook over a fire. These skills helped him all his life.

When Boone was 15, his family moved to the Yadkin Valley of North Carolina. Daniel led the group. For a few years, he helped his father farm, though he was never really interested in working the land. Hunting was his thing.

Daniel Boone

Dover Publications, Inc.

He served with General Braddock when he attacked the French Fort Duquesne. Boone drove a wagon, bringing up the rear of a four-mile column of soldiers. The French ambushed the British before they reached the fort. More than 900 British soldiers were killed or wounded. Braddock himself died in the battle. Boone and others left their wagons, jumped on horses, and barely escaped with their lives.

In 1756, Daniel Boone married Rebecca Bryant. Even though he was often gone for months at a time hunting, they had 10 children.

Boone was fascinated by stories of Kentucky he had heard from John Finley, who also fought with Braddock. In 1769, Boone, with his brother-in-law John Stewart and Finley, set off for Kentucky with a few other people and a dozen or so packhorses. After spending six months hunting in Kentucky, Boone decided to move his family there. During the trip, his oldest son, 16-year-old James, was killed by Indians. The Boones turned back and moved into a cabin on the Clinch River in Tennessee.

In 1775, Boone was hired to blaze a trail through the wilderness to Kentucky. They widened and leveled a Native American trail, the Warrior's Path, so wagons could use it.

The road went through the Cumberland Gap and into Kentucky. Boone built a large fort, later named Boonesborough, on the south side of the Kentucky River. The next year, he brought his family there to live.

Boone was captured by the Shawnee several times and adopted into their tribe. In September 1778 he escaped in time to warn Boonesborough of a coming Shawnee attack. The tribe laid siege to Boonesborough, setting fire to the fort after several days. Luckily a downpour of rain put out the fire, and the Shawnee gave up.

Through the years, Boone served in the Virginia legislature, was an innkeeper on the Ohio River, and worked as a deputy surveyor in Kentucky. After moving to Missouri, he was appointed *Syndic* of the area where he lived. This job combined the duties of judge, jury, and sheriff. Yet Boone was always happiest when he was hunting or trapping in the wilderness.

Boone tried to enlist in the Army during the War of 1812, and was furious when they turned him down because he was 78 years old. Rebecca died the next year, and in 1820, after being ill for a few weeks, Daniel Boone died.

The Northwest Territory

Both Massachusetts and New York once claimed what is now western New York. A treaty in 1786 divided the land between them. Massachusetts sold its share to Oliver Phelps and Nathaniel Gorham. (Phelps and Gorham also paid the Indians for much of the land, since they, too, claimed it.) The way was clear for Europeans to move into western New York.

The Northwest Ordinance in 1787 created the Northwest Territory. It was the land south of the Great Lakes, north and west of the Ohio River, and east of the Mississippi River. Several states would be created from this region. During the expansion of the United States, when an area had 60,000 people, it could become a state. In 1803, Ohio became the first state created from the territory.

The Louisiana Purchase and the Corps of Discovery

Exploration of the West really began with the Louisiana Purchase. Spain had sold its land in the New World to France in 1800. In 1803, Napoleon sold it to the United States, doubling the size of the country.

At this time there were few settlements in the far West. California had a few Spanish missions, and there was a settlement at Santa Fe. Some British and Russians had settlements along the Northwest Coast. They were made up of hunters and fur traders, but none of these groups was interested in making a permanent settlement.

The Louisiana Purchase included parts of what are now Oregon, Washington, Montana, Idaho, California, Nevada, Utah, New Mexico, Texas,

(left) **The new Northwest Territory and the states made from it.**

(right) **The Louisiana Purchase and the states made from it.**

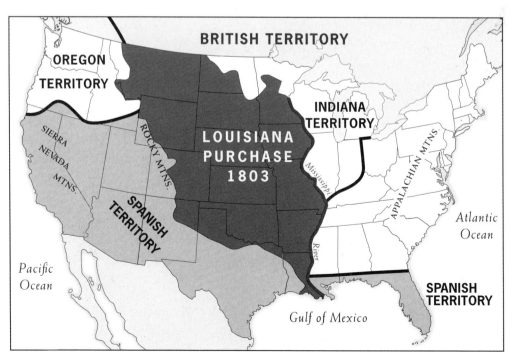

5

THOMAS JEFFERSON, 1743-1826

Thomas Jefferson, third president of the United States, was born on his family's plantation in Virginia in 1743. He attended the College of William and Mary. Starting in 1769, he served six years in the Virginia House of Burgesses, the colony's legislature.

In 1770, Jefferson began building a home of his own on land inherited from his father. He designed the building himself, and called it Monticello. It took many years to complete. Part of it was ready to live in by the time he married Martha Wayles Skelton, a widow, in 1772. Only two of their six children lived to be adults.

Jefferson was elected to the Second Continental Congress in 1776. They met in Philadelphia, where he was chosen to head the committee to write the Declaration of Independence. Jefferson did most of the writing, helped by John Adams and Benjamin Franklin.

During the American Revolution, Jefferson served in Virginia's new General Assembly. The war was still going on in June 1779 when he was elected governor of Virginia. He retired from the governorship in 1781. Martha Jefferson died the next year, and the year after that, Thomas Jefferson was again elected to Congress.

Jefferson's report on the establishment of a money unit for the United States led to the new country using the dollar, rather than the pound, which was used in England. Jefferson owned slaves but believed slavery was evil. His proposal to ban slavery in western territories after 1800 was narrowly defeated. A man who would have voted for it was at home sick, and the proposal lost by one vote.

From 1784 until 1789, Jefferson lived in France. He had been appointed minister to France, replacing Benjamin Franklin. In 1789, Jefferson returned to the United States when President Washington appointed him Secretary of State.

Jefferson finally resigned his position at the end of 1793. He retired to Monticello for three years. There he enjoyed the farm and his family, and his daughters and their children visited often. Jefferson experimented with inventions, remodeled Monticello, and planted a thousand peach trees.

Then in 1796 he reluctantly ran for president against John Adams. Adams won, and under the system at that time, Jefferson became vice president. In 1800, Jefferson ran again. He and Aaron Burr tied for the most votes, just ahead of John Adams. The House of Representatives had to break the tie, and they chose Jefferson to be president. During his term in office, one of his biggest accomplishments was negotiating with Napoleon to obtain the Louisiana Territory.

After his presidency, Jefferson founded the University of Virginia. He planned and designed the college. He also was in charge of construction and the hiring of faculty.

Jefferson died at Monticello on July 4, 1826, the 50th anniversary of the Declaration of Independence. John Adams died the same day.

Thomas Jefferson

Dover Publications, Inc.

Wyoming, and Colorado. The land was wilderness and had not been explored or mapped. It was populated with Native Americans and filled with buffalo, bears, wolves, and beavers. Mountain men and fur traders went into the area on their own. But within 50 years, the government and the U.S. Army had sent explorers and scouts to the area, and most of the land was explored. Pioneers began to settle in the West.

As they traveled, these explorers found wonderful scenic features including rivers, waterfalls, mountains, and lakes. They found deserts where they thought no one could live. They preserved their thoughts in letters, journals, and government reports.

In 1804, President Thomas Jefferson sent the first official expedition to explore the newly purchased land. He chose his private secretary, Meriwether Lewis, to head the group. Lewis asked his friend, William Clark, to join the expedition. Both kept daily journals we can still read today.

Jefferson's orders were to "explore the Missouri River and [find the] most direct and practical water communication across the continent, for the purposes of commerce." Lewis and Clark were also to map the area, see what natural resources were there, and try to make friends with the Indians.

On May 14, 1804, 29 men left the junction of the Mississippi and Missouri Rivers near present-day St. Louis. They started up the Missouri in a 55-foot keelboat. It had 22 oars and a sail. Two smaller boats, called *pirogues*, carried soldiers and rivermen. The rivermen were French Canadian experts who taught the men about travel on the river. As they traveled, Clark mapped the route while Lewis collected plant and animal specimens and made scientific observations. Several others on the trip also kept journals.

The trip was not easy. Where the current was too rough, they had to tow the boats from the shore. They camped and hunted for food. Huge clouds of mosquitoes swarmed around them. On a good day, they were able to go only 12 miles.

They met Indians from the Missouri, the Omaha, the Yankton Sioux, the Lakota, and the Arikara tribes. Lewis and Clark met with the chiefs, offering them gifts. They made speeches about peace. The only unfriendly tribe was the Lakota, who tried to take one of the explorers' canoes as payment for letting them use the river.

Lewis and Clark built a fort in what is now North Dakota, near the five Mandan Indian villages. The Indians were generous and friendly. Clark wrote in his journal, "This place we have named Fort Mandan in honour of our neighbours."

Lewis and Clark hired a French fur trader, Toussaint Charbonneau, as a guide. His Shoshone Indian wife, Sacagawea, would act as interpreter.

> **A French man by Name Chabonah, who Speaks the Big Belley language visit us he wished to hire & informed us his two squars [squaws] were Snake Indians, we engau [engaged] him to go on with us and take one of his wives to interpret the Snake language.**
>
> —*William Clark in his journal, November 4, 1804*

MERIWETHER LEWIS, 1774-1809

Meriwether Lewis was born on his family's plantation in Virginia in 1774. His father died when Lewis was only five years old. When Lewis was growing up, private tutors taught him, but he was also interested in the outdoors. He liked to hunt and explore. He eventually graduated from what is now Washington and Lee University.

Lewis joined the Virginia militia in 1794. That year he fought to put down the Whiskey Rebellion. Then the army sent him to the Northwest Territory in 1795 to fight against the Native Americans.

President Thomas Jefferson was an old friend. In 1801 he asked Lewis to be his private secretary. Jefferson hoped to buy a large parcel of land west of the Mississippi. He was already planning to explore that land and wanted Lewis to lead an expedition, called the Corps of Discovery. To prepare him,

Meriwether Lewis

Dover Publications, Inc.

Jefferson sent Lewis to the University of Pennsylvania. There he studied plants, animals, minerals, the stars, and medicine. Lewis was to plan and organize the expedition. He would obtain all the supplies, too.

Lewis chose William Clark as his co-leader. He had served in the U.S. Army with Clark and trusted him. Meanwhile, Jefferson and Congress bought the Louisiana Territory from France in April 1803.

Lewis and Clark set off the next May on their expedition. Lewis's studies proved very helpful. He collected and identified many plants and animals. When the men returned, Jefferson appointed Lewis governor of the Louisiana Territory. He also asked him to write the official account of the expedition.

Lewis turned out to be a poor administrator. He argued with local leaders and didn't inform Jefferson of his decisions and policies. In 1809, he was called to the capital to answer complaints. He left Louisiana in September, but never made it to Washington. On October 11 he stopped at an inn about 70 miles from Nashville, Tennessee. The next morning, he was found dead in his room. Many people, including Jefferson, thought he committed suicide. His family and others believed he was murdered. No one knows for certain which theory is true.

⟜ WILLIAM CLARK, 1779–1838 ⟜

William Clark was born on the family plantation in Virginia, the ninth of ten children. When he was 14, the family moved to the Louisville, Kentucky, area. Although his family was wealthy, he had no formal education.

In 1789, Clark joined the militia and went to fight the Native Americans in the Ohio Valley. He joined the regular army in 1792, served under General Anthony Wayne, and in 1794 commanded a company at the Battle of Fallen Timbers. Clark's riflemen drove back the Indians and Canadians on the left flank, earning Wayne's thanks.

Clark retired from the Army in 1796. He went home to manage Mulberry Hill, his plantation near Louisville. In 1803, his old army friend, Meriwether Lewis, asked him to share his command on an expedition. The group would explore the new Louisiana Territory. To get ready for the trip, Clark studied astronomy and *cartography*—map-making. On the expedition, he made the maps and planned the routes. He also kept the records and managed supplies.

When the Corps of Discovery returned from its expedition, Jefferson appointed Clark chief Indian agent for the Louisiana Territory. Clark married Julia Hancock in 1807, and they had five children. After Lewis's death in 1809, Clark had to edit the expedition's journals for publication.

In 1813, Clark became governor of the Missouri Territory. He lost the election for governor when Missouri became a state in 1820. Julia died that same year, and he married her cousin, Harriet Kennerly Radford. They had three more children.

In 1822 President James Monroe appointed Clark Superintendent of Indian Affairs. He kept that job until his death in 1838. Both Native Americans and European Americans remembered Clark for his fairness and honesty.

William Clark

Dover Publications, Inc.

BISON

The American bison has been the largest land mammal in North America since the end of the Ice Age. The huge animals can weigh as much as a ton. Most people call them buffalo. The Native Americans and buffalo lived together for thousands of years. The Plains Indians hunted the buffalo, but took only as many as they needed and didn't waste any part of the animal. They ate the meat immediately or preserved it to eat later. They used the hides for clothing and tents. *Sinews*—intestines—were used as thread, and needles and tools were made from the bones.

There were at least 30 million buffalo roaming North America before the Europeans came. Some people believe there were as many as 70 million. As the Europeans settled the East, the buffalo moved farther west. While the West was being settled, buffalo were slaughtered by the millions. Most were shot by hunters as sport. Some even shot at the animals from the windows of moving trains.

Most bison were killed between 1830 and 1880. According to the National Park Service, there were no wild bison left in the United States by 1883. By 1900, there were fewer than 600 left, but they were protected. Conservationists managed to save those buffalo. Those you see today are their descendants.

Today, bison are raised on ranches and farms for meat. Between Canada and the United States, there are about 500,000 bison in North America. About 20,000 roam on public lands and preserves in the two countries. The 4,000 bison in Yellowstone National Park make up the largest herd of free-roaming plains bison. Wood Buffalo National Park in Canada has the most free-roaming wood bison. That herd has about 10,000 animals.

Shooting bison from a train.

Library of Congress LC-USZ62-133890

In the spring, a few men headed back to report to Jefferson. They took Native American items, soil and mineral samples, and plants. They even took a prairie dog and some live birds. The rest of the group continued their trek west.

On their way to what is now Montana, they saw a lot of wildlife. Wolves, buffalo, grizzly bears, and bighorn sheep were abundant.

At the headwaters of the Missouri, the group visited a Shoshone village. Sacagawea was amazed to find that her brother, whom she hadn't seen for years, was the chief. She was able to obtain horses for the expedition to use to cross the mountains.

Jefferson had thought the expedition would be near the Pacific by September 1804, because he believed there was only a small mountain range to the west of the Great Plains, with a river to the Pacific. Actually, it took the group 11 days to cross the Bitterroot Mountains, in what is now Idaho. They were already covered with snow in September, and the Corps nearly starved.

On the other side of the mountains, they met Nez Perce Indians, who helped them make canoes, provided them with food, and offered to keep their horses while they were gone.

After floating down the Clearwater, Snake, and Columbia Rivers, the expedition finally reached the Pacific early in November. It had taken them a year and a half. They spent a cold, wet, miserable winter near where Astoria, Oregon, is today.

The long journey home began on March 23, 1806. The party split into two groups and explored other territory on the way back. The only violent encounter with native tribes happened to Lewis's group. Blackfeet Indians tried to steal their horses and guns, and Lewis's men killed two of them.

Clark was on a route to the south and found a large stone formation on the Yellowstone River. He named it "Pompy's Tower," for Sacagawea's baby boy. Clark carved his name and the date. The inscription can still be seen today.

The two groups met on the Missouri River at the mouth of the Yellowstone and then continued east together. The expedition reached St. Louis on September 23, 1806.

Lewis and Clark were greeted as heroes. Many people had thought they were dead because they had been gone so long. Yet only one man, Charles Floyd, had died on the trip.

With their return, the government knew a great deal more about the new territory. It now had the maps that Clark made. The expedition had brought back information on the people, the rivers, the mountains, and the plants and animals in the West.

CRADLEBOARDS

Most Native American tribes used cradleboards to carry their babies. A cradleboard took the place of the car seats, infant carriers, and cradles we have today.

The mother carried the baby on her back while she was working. Sometimes she propped the cradleboard up against a wall. If she rode a horse, she would hang the cradleboard from the saddle. Native Americans thought the cradleboard made the babies feel safe and loved because they were always close to their mothers. Many mothers today wear slings to carry their babies close to their bodies.

When strapped to a cradleboard, the baby usually couldn't move its arms and legs. Sometimes the top laces were loosened so the baby could move its arms around. The Indians believed the babies developed strong neck and back muscles and good posture from being in the cradleboard.

Babies were often wrapped in furs or soft moss before being put into the cradleboard. It had a flat, hard back, which protected the baby's head. Either animal skin or cloth was arranged to cover the baby's head in bad weather or bright sunshine. Animal hides were used to make the flaps, which laced together in the front. Most cradleboards were decorated with beads or quills.

Sometimes a mother made her cradleboard, but it was usually made by a grandmother or an aunt. Some Native Americans still use cradleboards for their babies.

When you know of a child being born, then you prepare. You start making their clothes. We get the baby boards ready, and we have to keep to tradition. When a baby board is made, it has to be made in a day. You begin at the break of day and it has to be done before evening so the child will grow up to be a good person.
—*Sophie George, descendant of the Yakama and Colville tribes in Oregon*

Sacagawea carried her baby, Pompy, on a cradleboard similar to this child's.

Library of Congress LC-USZ62-97090

SACAGAWEA, 1788-1812

Sacagawea was born into the Shoshone tribe in what is now Idaho. When she was twelve years old, the Hidatsa Indians kidnapped her. Some sources believe she was sold as a slave to Toussaint Charbonneau, a French-Canadian fur trader in early 1804, but others say the Hidatsa did not practice slavery. However it happened, she married Charbonneau when she was about 15 years old.

The Lewis and Clark Expedition hired Charbonneau and Sacagawea to travel with them as translators. That fall, the expedition party built Fort Mandan in what is now South Dakota. That winter at the fort, Sacagawea gave birth to a baby boy. She named him Jean-Baptiste Charbonneau. Pompy was his nickname.

In the spring, the expedition continued west. Lewis and Clark knew they would meet Shoshones on the way and wanted Sacagawea to translate for them, though she spoke no English. She talked to the Shoshones in their language, and then translated their remarks into Hidatsa. Charbonneau understood Hidatsa and translated into French. Francois Labiche, part of the expedition, spoke French, and could translate Charbonneau's remarks into English for Lewis and Clark.

The presence of an Indian woman and child reassured other Native Americans that this was not a war party. Sacagawea also helped in other ways. She found roots and berries for the group to eat, showed them how to make leather moccasins and clothing, and cooked for them. And when a canoe capsized, she managed to save many important papers, earning her the praise of Lewis and Clark.

When they met a group of Shoshone, Sacagawea was amazed to recognize the chief as her brother, Cameahwait. She hadn't seen him for five years, since the Hidatsa had kidnapped her.

There are legends that Sacagawea was the chief guide on the expedition, but most historians don't believe that. However, Lewis and Clark considered her an important part of the expedition. When they voted on where to stay for the winter, they gave her an equal vote with the leaders.

After the expedition, Sacagawea went with her husband to Fort Manuel on the Missouri River. In 1812, she gave birth to a daughter. Soon after, she died, at the age of 25.

Eight months later, William Clark legally adopted both Jean-Baptiste and the baby, Lisette. He educated the boy in St. Louis, and then sent him to Europe for more schooling. There is no record of Lisette after her adoption.

Sacagawea was recently honored when a new gold dollar coin was introduced featuring her likeness. Actually, no pictures of her exist, so the portrait on the coin may not look like her, though it does honor her for her accomplishments.

The Sacagawea gold dollar coin recognizes her value to the Corps of Discovery.

MAKE A TEPEE

Plains Indians like Sacagawea lived in tepees made from hides, usually buffalo skins. The skin was put over four wooden poles to hold it up. Most tepees were decorated with symbols and designs. Because you can't get buffalo skins, your tepee will be made from brown paper.

What You Need

Brown grocery bag
Scissors
Dinner plate
Crayons or markers
Glue
Four twigs, each about 6 inches long
Short piece of yarn or string

Cut out a piece of brown paper from the bag. Make sure it is bigger than the plate.

Lay the dinner plate on the paper and trace around it. Then cut out the circle.

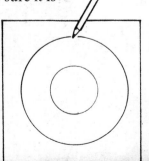

Fold the circle in half and cut along the fold line. You could share the other half with a partner, as you'll only need one half-circle.

Before you assemble the tepee, decorate the paper with Native American symbols and designs. You can find these in books or on the Internet.

Overlap the flat edges of your tepee to form a cone. Glue together. After the glue has dried, snip off the very top of the cone for the twigs to stick through.

Tie your twigs loosely together about an inch from the top with yarn or string. Spread them out.

Set your tepee down over the sticks, letting them stick out at the top. If the twigs are too long on the bottom, trim them off.

Cut a slit about two inches long in one side of the tepee. Fold it back to make a flap door.

13

Another Western Expedition

Before Lewis and Clark returned from the West, Zebulon Pike set off on a mission. In 1805, General James Wilkinson sent Pike to find the source of the Mississippi River, but didn't inform Jefferson of the expedition.

Pike's official instructions said to make peace treaties with the native tribes in the area. He was also to take note of the "geographical structure, natural history, and population" of the land he traveled through. And he was to "avoid giving offense to the Spanish," since he would be near their territory.

Wilkinson told him unofficially that he was on a spy mission. He was to find out the size, strength, and location of Spanish forces in and near the Louisiana Territory. However, Pike didn't know that Wilkinson was working as a secret agent for the Spanish.

Pike obtained horses from the Osage Indians after spending three weeks with them. He and his group followed the Kansas River, then the Arkansas. In November the party reached what is now Colorado. They discovered a tall mountain peak that Pike decided was unclimbable. It is today known as Pikes Peak.

Pike became lost after following the South Platte River for a distance. His men spent Christmas week lost in Royal Gorge. They finally made their way out on Pike's birthday. He said he "hope[d] never to pass another so miserably." They nearly starved to death during the freezing weather. They finally killed a buffalo, which likely saved the expedition. On January 30, 1807, they arrived at the Rio Grande. There they built a small *stockade*, or fort.

One hundred Spanish soldiers appeared at the stockade near the end of February. The commanding officer said, "Sir, the governor of New Mexico, being informed you had missed your route, ordered me to offer you, in his name, mules, horses, money, or whatever you may . . . need . . . to conduct you to the head of the Red River."

He escorted them to Santa Fe, where they were given supplies and sent home through the Mexican territory of Texas. The expedition arrived home in July 1807.

Pike's trip was important because he was the first to explore some of the land in the southwestern part of the Louisiana Territory. The men also blazed much of what became the Santa Fe Trail.

Pikes Peak
© *histcreatr*

Trappers, Hunters, and Mountain Men

Others were also heading west, but many were not interested in exploring or settling there. These were the fur trappers, hunters, and mountain men.

John Jacob Astor, a rich and famous fur merchant, sent a group west in 1811. Wilson Hunt led the group. Astor sent another group by water to land on the Pacific Coast of Oregon.

Hunt's group went on horseback as far as Montana. The land became rugged, and water was scarce. The men had to go south into the Laramie Mountains of Wyoming. On the way, they passed Devils Tower.

Crow Indians helped Hunt's group cross the Bighorn Mountains. They continued west, past the Grand Teton Mountains, then stopped at the Snake River to build canoes. Two Snake Indians came into camp and told them the river was too rough for canoes, but the explorers didn't believe it until they sent out a scouting party. They came back and said it would be impossible to canoe down the river.

(top) **Trappers relax around their campfire.**
Library of Congress LC-DIG-pga-00935

(bottom) **Devils Tower is an easily recognized landmark.**
Library of Congress LC-DIG-ppmsc-02645

ZEBULON PIKE, 1779-1813

Zebulon Pike is best known for discovering Pikes Peak in Colorado, which is named for him. He was born in New Jersey in 1779. When he was 15, Pike joined the army. By 1799, he was a first lieutenant.

Pike married Clarissa Brown in 1801. They were stationed at several frontier posts. In 1805, General James Wilkinson ordered Pike to find the source of the Mississippi River. He believed he had found it when he reached Leech Lake in what is now Minnesota.

After he returned from that journey, Pike led an expedition in the Southwest.

He was to find the sources of the Arkansas and Red Rivers. When Pike and his team reached what is now New Mexico, they were captured by the Spanish. The Spanish took them to Santa Fe, and later to Chihuahua in Mexico. After appearing before government officials there, they were escorted back to the United States frontier.

Pike published an account of his Southwest expedition in 1810. His writing influenced exploration and settlement in the area. His descriptions helped promote the development of the Santa Fe Trail.

Pike later became a military agent in New Orleans, and fought in the War of 1812. He was killed by flying rock during one of its battles when the British blew up the Americans' ammunition store.

Zebulon Pike

Dover Publications, Inc.

Two Snake Indians guided them to Fort Henry, which had been abandoned. They again built canoes and attempted to navigate the river. After losing a man in the rapids, they gave up on the canoes. During that winter, they were forced to kill and eat one of their horses to keep from starving. They finally got to Astoria, Oregon, on February 15. The group that had sailed was already waiting for them.

Hunt's expedition was important. It showed that the way Lewis and Clark went was not the only way across the Rockies. This expedition was the first to see the Laramie Mountains and to come through the Wind River Mountains by way of Union Pass. They were also the first to cross the Tetons and the Blue Mountains in southeast Oregon.

Long's Expeditions

Major Stephen Long led the first scientific exploration up the Platte River. On June 6, 1820, Long left Council Bluffs, Nebraska, with 21 men. They followed the Platte to the Rockies. A mountain peak there was later named Longs Peak. Some of the expedition also climbed Pikes Peak. The explorers went south, looking for the Red River, which formed part of the boundary with Mexico. They followed the Canadian River, thinking it was the Red River. When they learned of their mistake, they went east from New Mexico to the Texas Panhandle. They were the first American expedition to cross the Panhandle.

Long reported that the Plains from Nebraska to Oklahoma were "unfit for cultivation and of course uninhabitable by a people depending upon agriculture." On the map he drew, he labeled the Great Plains area "Great Desert." For years, settlers avoided the area.

In 1823, Long led an expedition to explore the sources of the Minnesota and Red Rivers in the north. They also explored the U.S.-Canadian boundary west of the Great Lakes.

The Santa Fe Trail

In September 1821, William Becknell and four other men left Missouri to go west. They took many mules loaded with cotton to sell. On November 13, they met a number of Mexican soldiers. They took the group on to Santa Fe, where they were welcomed. They made a great profit on their cotton.

Becknell led a *wagon train*, several wagons traveling together, to Santa Fe the next year. Three wagons, 21 men, and 24 oxen left Missouri on May 22. They had more problems this time. It was a rainy spring, and the heavy wagons sunk in the mud. Each loaded wagon weighed 7,000 pounds, and they made slow progress. But an encounter with 1,000 Osage Indians turned out well after Becknell talked to the chiefs and gave them gifts.

Other problems were a lack of firewood and too little water as they crossed the desert. They finally made it to Santa Fe.

After crossing a mountainous country, we arrived at Santa Fe and were received with apparent pleasure and joy. It is situated in a valley of the mountains on a branch of the Rio del Norte [Rio Grande River]. Their atmosphere is remarkably dry and rain is uncommon, except in the months of July and August. . . . Their domestic animals consist chiefly of sheep, goat, mules, and asses. None but the wealthy have horses and hogs. . . . The walls of their houses are two or three feet thick, built of sun-dried brick [and have] a flat roof made of clay and floors of the same material.

—*William Becknell*

Becknell is referred to as the "Father of the Santa Fe Trail," since he found a way to take a wagon train from Missouri to Santa Fe. The trail was the main road between the United States and Mexico for 25 years. At the end of the Mexican American War, the land became part of the United States.

More Discoveries

Jim Bridger, a fur trapper in the Rocky Mountains, found Great Salt Lake in 1824. Some believe he was the first man of European descent to see the lake; others think Etienne Provost was. Because of the salt water, they believed the lake was an arm of the Pacific Ocean.

Years later, in 1850, Bridger found a pass through the Rockies. It became known as Bridger's Pass. The Union Pacific Railroad was built through this pass. Interstate 80 now goes through the pass. In 1859–60 he visited "Colter's Hell," which had been discovered by John Colter in 1807. Bridger described the geysers and other thermal wonders there, in what is now Yellowstone National Park. No one believed him.

NATIVE AMERICANS IN YOUR STATE

No matter where you live in the United States, there were Indians living in your state at one time. Just think, a Native American boy or girl might have lived right where your house is today.

In the East, there were Woodland Indians. They usually lived in the forests in houses called wigwams or longhouses. They used canoes and hunted deer.

Plains Indians lived throughout the Great Plains area. These were the Indians that the settlers had the most conflicts with. That's because the wagon trains passed through their hunting grounds. Most of them lived in tepees. By the time the Westward Movement began, the Plains Indians were using horses.

The Pueblo Indians lived in the Southwest. They lived in "apartment houses" built of adobe or clay bricks. Since they usually stayed in one spot, they grew food in gardens.

And in Florida, the Seminole Indians lived in much of the state. They lived in homes called *chickees*, built on platforms. They used boats and hunted alligators.

Try to find out more about the Native Americans in the state where you live. If you can use the Internet, do a search. If you aren't able to go online, you can go to the library and look for books on Native Americans. Find out what Indians lived where you do. Learn about the food they ate, the clothes they wore, and the houses they lived in.

◄◄ ◄►►

2
The Trip West

Pioneers moved west for many reasons. Often they had little money and wanted a new start. Farmers heard of rich land in the West that was cheaper than land in the East. Later, when homesteading began, settlers could even get land for free.

Others thought the East was getting too crowded—they didn't like having neighbors so close. It was said Daniel Boone believed when he could see the smoke from another cabin's chimney, it was time to move on.

Many hunters and trappers headed west. Game animals in the East became harder to find as civilization drove them from the area. But most hunters and trappers didn't take their families with them when they went west.

Some people went west to avoid the Civil War. Others were fleeing from the law. This number included runaway slaves who feared they would be returned to their owners if they stayed in the East.

Some went for their health. They believed the climate in Oregon and other western destinations would be healthier. Unfortunately, many pioneers died on the trail.

Some pioneers went west in 1849 as part of the Gold Rush. On January 24, 1848, James Marshall discovered lumps of gold at John Sutter's Mill in California. Nine days later, on February 2, California became a U.S. territory.

News traveled slowly in those days. The San Francisco newspaper *The Californian* reported the gold strike on March 15, 1849. Many people did not believe it, but in San Francisco on May 12, a man named Sam Brannan waved a bottle of gold dust and yelled, "Gold! Gold! Gold from the American River!" Gold fever had begun! People already in California rushed to Sutter's Mill, hoping to get rich.

The whole country from San Francisco to Los Angeles, and from the sea shore to the base of the Sierra Nevadas, resounds with the sordid cry of gold, GOLD, GOLD! While the field is left half-planted, the house half-built, and everything neglected but the manufacture of shovels and pickaxes.

—The Californian, *May 29, 1849*

Pioneers have stopped for the night and drawn their wagons in a circle.

Library of Congress LC-USZ62-133213

The newspaper also announced it was stopping publication, since most of the staff had left for the gold fields.

It took longer for the news of gold to reach the East. On December 5, President James Polk confirmed that gold had been discovered in California.

> **The accounts of abundance of gold are of such an extraordinary character as would scarcely command belief were they not corroborated [supported] by the authentic reports of officers in the public service.**
>
> —*President James Polk*

By the end of December 1848, the population of San Francisco had grown from 459 people (in 1847) to 100,000. About 43,000 people had come in wagons and another 35,000 had come by sea. At that time, it was necessary to sail all the way around the southern tip of South America to get from the East Coast to California by ship. It was a long, dangerous voyage and took five to eight months.

With the rapid population growth came problems with law and order. Zachary Taylor, who became president early in 1849, recommended California be given statehood so the government could protect people and keep the peace. Taylor died in office, and Millard Fillmore became president, but on September 9, 1850, California became a free state. That meant slavery was not allowed within its borders.

It soon became obvious that a railroad was needed to run from the Mississippi River to California. The trip overland by wagon was grueling, and the trip by boat took too long.

President James Polk
Dover Publications, Inc.

THE TREATY ⊷ OF ⊷ GUADALUPE HIDALGO

In 1845, Texas became part of the United States. Texas was once part of Mexico, but the Texans revolted in 1836 and declared their independence. In 1846, Mexicans attacked U.S. troops on the south border of Texas. The two countries fought until September 14, 1847, when U.S. General Winfield Scott occupied Mexico City, ending the war. As a result, the Treaty of Guadalupe Hidalgo was signed in 1848. It recognized that Texas was part of the United States, and also ceded California and New Mexico (which included Arizona) to the United States.

A transcontinental railroad was discussed for several years, but Northerners and Southerners couldn't agree on the route. When the South seceded from the union in 1861, it was clear there would be a northern route. President Abraham Lincoln signed the Pacific Railroad Act in 1862. The Central Pacific Railroad would start building tracks east from Sacramento. The Union Pacific Railroad would start in Omaha, Nebraska, and build west. The railroad followed an old pioneer trail.

More than 20,000 people worked to build the tracks. Most were immigrants. Almost 10,000 Chinese laborers worked for the Central Pacific. The Union Pacific hired Irish, German, Dutch, and Eastern European workers. The railroads also employed several thousand Civil War veterans.

Both companies' laborers worked under brutal conditions. The Union Pacific workers had to worry about Indian attacks, outlaws, summer heat, and long 12-hour shifts. The Central Pacific's shifts were just as long. They also worked under dangerous conditions through mountainous terrain. In the winter, an avalanche could strike at any moment. Sometimes whole crews were swept down a mountainside and buried. Black powder and nitroglycerine, explosives used to clear the way for the railroad, sometimes exploded too soon, injuring or killing workers.

Both companies were hurrying their workers, wanting to get to Salt Lake City first. Amazingly, no point had been named for the two sets of tracks to meet. Therefore, they passed each other in northern Utah. Congress finally made them agree on a meeting point: Promontory, Utah. The two sets of tracks were joined there on May 10, 1869. It had taken six years of backbreaking work, but California was finally connected by railroad to the rest of the United States.

The Union Pacific and Central Pacific finally meet in Utah.

Library of Congress LC-USZ62-116354

Trails West

During the Western Migration, pioneers used many forms of transportation. Some traveled in boats, some took trains, and a few rode horses. In later years, some people traveled west on stagecoaches. Two-wheeled handcarts were sometimes used. They required no animals to pull them. However, the owner had to walk the entire way, pulling the cart. A few hardy pioneers walked the whole trail, carrying their belongings in backpacks. But the most common method of travel was by covered wagon.

Wagons could be pulled by horses, mules, or oxen. Most pioneers used oxen. They were stronger and could live on the grass they found along the trail. Horses were faster, but they needed feed and they couldn't pull as heavy a load. Some travelers used mules. They were stronger than horses, but they also had to be fed grain. They were sometimes bad-tempered, too. Oxen were also better in sand and mud, and Native Americans didn't want to steal them.

Your wagons should be light, yet substantial and strong, and plenty of good oxen. . . . Have your wagon beds made in such a manner that they can be used for boats; you will find them of great service in crossing streams . . . have your wagons well covered, so that they will not leak or your provisions and clothes will spoil.

—*S. M. Gilmore, who traveled the Oregon Trail in 1843*

BE A MODERN-DAY PIONEER

Suppose you found out that you were moving to a new place without electricity. All your family can take is what will fit in a small rental trailer. (Not a moving van!) Think about what things you think the family should take. Make a list of the most important things. Remember clothing, food, books, toys, tools, and furniture. But remember, computers, video games, and TVs won't work. Given how little room you have in the trailer, what other things will you have to leave behind?

➤ PRAIRIE SCHOONERS ➤

Most pioneers did not use the Conestoga wagons used in the East because they were too large and heavy for the trail. Animals couldn't pull the big Conestoga wagons all the way across the country. The wagons most pioneers used, called *prairie schooners*, looked a lot like the Conestoga wagons. They used the same design but were smaller and lighter—a prairie schooner was about half the size of a Conestoga wagon.

The prairie schooners were about four feet wide and 10 to 12 feet long. Four to seven wooden hoops, called *bows*, were bent and fastened to the sides of the wagon. They formed a roof when canvas was stretched across the bows. The canvas was oiled to make it waterproof, and could be closed in front and back by drawstrings in case of a storm.

Inside the wagon, hooks hung from the bows. They were used to hang clothing, weapons, and other items. Some wagons had springs to smooth out the ride, but only in the front. Even so, it was a rough and bumpy way to travel. In good weather, most people walked alongside the wagon.

Some people just used their farm wagons, and built bows and covered them. These wagons were usually smaller than those built especially for the trip.

Covered wagons such as this were used for the trip west.

© Hofmeester

When a family decided to go west, there was a lot of planning to do. They had to figure out the best time to leave. The trip would take several months, so they usually set off in spring. But they needed to wait until the snow melted. If they had oxen, they would need to eat the grass along the way.

> Through all the winter preceding the April morning when the final start was made, the fingers of the women and girls were busy providing additional stores of bedding and blankets, of stockings and sunbonnets, of hickory shirts and gingham aprons. Ah! The tears that fell upon these garments, fashioned with trembling fingers by the flaring light of tallow candles, the heartaches that were stitched and knitted and woven into them, throughout the brief winter afternoons, as relatives that were to be left behind and friends of a lifetime dropped in to lend a hand in the awesome undertaking of getting ready for a journey that promised no return.
>
> —*Catherine "Kit" Scott, age 13 in 1852*

Enough food had to be packed to last the whole family for the entire journey. Most families' lists included flour, bacon, baking soda, corn meal, hardtack, dried beans, dried beef, dried fruit, molasses, vinegar, pepper, eggs, salt, sugar, rice, and tea.

The wagon also held bedding, clothing, tents, weapons, cooking utensils, a chamber pot, a washbowl, a lantern, candle molds, needles and thread, and tools such as an ax, a hammer, a hoe, a plow, and a shovel.

Many of the pioneers had to sell a house or farm before they could set off on their westward journey. Some also had to make arrangements for someone to care for aging parents or children left behind. And when the day came to leave, all the neighbors usually turned out to say good-bye.

> **The last hours were spent in bidding good-bye to old friends. My mother is heartbroken over this separation of relatives and friends. Giving up old associations for what? Good health, perhaps. The last good-bye has been said—the last glimpse of our old home on the hill, and wave a hand at the old Academy, with a good-bye to kind teachers and schoolmates, and we are off.**
>
> —*Sallie Hester, age 14 in 1849*

Some children were unhappy because they had to leave their pets behind.

> **We took a last look at our dear homestead as it faded from our view. We looked back and saw our old watch dog, his name was Watch, howling on the distant shore. Father had driven him back, saying, "Go back to Grandfather, Watch!" but he never ate afterwards, and soon died.**
>
> —*Etty Scott, age 11 in 1852*

An ox yoke was made of wood.
Photo by author, courtesy Garst Museum, Greenville, Ohio

Rather than travel alone, the family traveled in a line with other wagons for safety. A group of wagons was less likely to be attacked by Indians. And if someone was hurt or became ill, there were others to help. In the evenings, pioneers enjoyed the company of the others in the wagon train.

After a few days, the travelers became used to life on the trail. It took on a sort of routine. They got up early, started a fire, cooked breakfast, ate, and repacked the wagons. The animals were hitched to the wagons, and the wagon train was on its way again.

The men usually walked alongside the oxen. The oxen wore wooden yokes, and there were no reins with which to drive them. Children usually walked most of the way in good weather. Around noon, the wagons would stop. Everyone would spend an hour or so eating lunch and resting. Then it was back on the trail again.

On a good day, the wagons would travel 10 to 15 miles. Around 5 o'clock, the wagon train usually stopped for the night. The wagons were drawn up in a circle, to help protect them from Indian attack. The livestock was corralled inside the circle of wagons. After dinner, people often

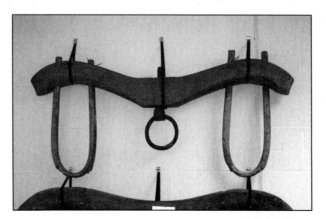

sat around a campfire and talked, sang, danced, or told stories. There was usually not room for a whole family to sleep in the wagon. So most of the people slept in tents, under the wagons, or outside under the stars.

Everyone had jobs to do along the trail, even the children. They would fetch water from a stream, watch the smaller children, help unpack bedding and cooking utensils, help cook and wash dishes, and hunt for firewood or buffalo chips. *Buffalo chips* were large, flat pieces of dry dung that burned well.

Trouble Along the Trail

Unfortunately, all days on the trail didn't go smoothly. The pioneers faced many hardships on their trip west. Nature had many surprises in store along the way. In dry weather, dust was a big problem. If your wagon was near the end of the line, you were forced to breathe the dust kicked up by the other wagons. Many people walked off to the side of the trail to avoid the worst of the dust. Often their eyes became red and swollen, and their lips were cracked.

Usually each wagon was assigned a certain position in the line. Each day, the wagon that had been first the day before would go to the end of the line. The others would move up. That way no one had to breathe the dust all the time.

Walking could be tiring and dusty, but riding in the wagon could cause trouble, too.

> Not being accustomed to riding in a covered wagon, the motion made us all sick, and the uncomfortableness of the situation was increased from the fact that it had set into rain, which made it impossible to roll back the cover and let in the fresh air. It also caused a damp and musty smell that was very nauseating. It took several weeks of travel to overcome this "sea sickness."
>
> —*Catherine Sager, age 13 in 1844*

Members of a wagon train relaxing around a campfire in the evening.
Library of Congress LC-USZ62-133214

Most of the trails followed rivers. Sometimes the water along the way was not fit to drink. Often earlier travelers left notes on rocks or pieces of wood, warning that the water was poisonous. To make it drinkable, sometimes pioneers boiled the water, mixed it with powdered charcoal, or filtered it through a handkerchief. Boiling might kill the germs and parasites, but the other methods merely made it clearer.

Weather caused many problems. It was hard to travel during a downpour. Rain accompanied by high wind could tear the canvas off a wagon. Even if the top stayed on, wind could blow rain into the wagon, soaking clothing and bedding.

After the rain, the pioneers had to cope with mud and quicksand. Also, heavy rains often caused swollen streams that were difficult to cross. Lightning even killed several people on their way west.

Wind could blow down trees, which would block the trail. Then the pioneers had to take time to remove the obstacles. When it was hot, people needed more water to drink. Some travelers left too late in the spring and were caught by early snows.

Often the travelers were plagued by insects. Mosquitoes, chiggers, ticks, lice, gnats, fleas, and flies were common.

The pioneers' limited diet was also a problem. Lack of fresh fruits and vegetables could cause a condition called *scurvy*. It was difficult to get fresh produce, but most pioneers carried pickles on the trail. They also packed dried fruit.

Lack of sufficient shoes and clothing became a problem late in their trips. Shoes wore out as the trip went on. May Ellen Murdock Compton

Pioneers bring a wagon across the Platte River.
Library of Congress
LC-DIG-ppmsc-04815

wrote in her diary that she left Independence, Missouri, with ten new pairs of shoes. She wore out nine pairs on the Oregon Trail. Then she walked the last few miles barefoot because she wanted to save the last pair of shoes to wear in her new Oregon home.

Women and girls found it difficult to walk through grass and weeds when wearing long dresses. Some wore bloomers, which were long, full pants.

Our clothing is light and durable. My sister and I wear short dresses and bloomers and our foot gear includes a pair of light calf-skin topboots for wading through the mud and sand.

—Eliza Ann McAuley, age 17 in 1852

Brothers George and Jacob Donner organized a party of emigrants to go to California in 1846. The Reed family was included. Thirty-two people left Springfield, Illinois, on April 16 that year. They expected to reach San Francisco in about four months. Others joined them along the way.

The Donner Party had problems from the beginning. Thunderstorms caused deep mud, making it hard going for the oxen and wagons. They were lucky to travel two miles some days.

At Fort Laramie, the Donner Party met James Clyman, an old friend of James Reed. Reed shared the Donner Party's plan with Clyman. Further down the trail, at Fort Bridger, they planned to take a shortcut recommended by Lansford Hastings. He had

written *The Emigrants' Guide to Oregon and California*. In it, he mentioned the shortest way would be "to leave the Oregon route about two hundred miles east of Fort Hall; thence bearing west-southwest to the Salt Lake; and thence continuing down to the bay of San Francisco." He claimed it would cut 300 to 400 miles off the trip. He also said the way was smooth and level, and there was no danger from Indians.

Clyman warned Reed to take the longer route, saying the wagons could not make it through the pass. Reed and George Donner, the captains of the wagon train, decided to try the Hastings Cut-Off anyway.

The Donner Party expected to meet Hastings at Fort Bridger and thought he would guide them through the shortcut. By the time they arrived, Hastings had already left with another wagon train. They thought they could catch up with him. James Reed and two others rode ahead and talked with Hastings. He refused to return, but pointed out the general direction of the shortcut.

Donner Lake in the Sierra Nevadas, near where the Donners camped.

Library of Congress LC-USZ62-27617

There was absolutely no road, not even a trail. The canyon wound around among the hills. Heavy underbrush had to be cut away and used for making a road bed. While cutting our way step-by-step through the "Hastings Cut-Off" we were overtaken and joined by the Graves family. . . . Finally we reached the end of the canyon where it looked as though our wagons would have to be abandoned. It seemed impossible for the oxen to pull them up the steep hill and the bluffs beyond, but we doubled teams and the work was, at last, accomplished, almost every yoke in the train being required to pull up each wagon.

—*Virginia Reed, age 12*

In 21 days on the Hastings Cut-Off, the group had moved only 35 miles. They were running out of food. The group finally reached Great Salt Lake a month after leaving the main trail. They camped in a valley called Twenty Wells, where there was plenty of pure, cold water.

Then they set off across the Salt Plain in the evening. They traveled all night, all day, and all the next night. The nights were numbingly cold, and during the day they suffered from heat and thirst. Some of the oxen died, and some families had to abandon their wagons.

It took them five days to cross the desert. When they reached the other side, they took stock of their food. They had 600 miles to go and knew the provisions wouldn't last that long. A dusting of snow covered the mountain peaks that night.

C. T. Stanton and William McCutchen rode off to Sutter's Fort to get provisions. The rest of the party moved on. Stanton and two Native American cowboys met them along the Truckee River with seven mules loaded with food. McCutchen was ill, so he stayed behind at the fort.

It was late October when the party started climbing the Sierra Nevada Mountains. Snow began to fall.

When it was seen that the wagons could not be dragged through the snow, their goods and provisions were packed on oxen and another start was made, men and women walking in the snow up to their waists, carrying their children in their arms and trying to drive their cattle. The Indians said they could find no road, so a halt was called, and Stanton went ahead with the guides, and came back and reported that we could get across if we kept right on, but that it would be impossible if snow fell. He was in favor of a forced march until the other side of the summit should be reached, but some of our party were so tired and exhausted with the day's labor that they declared they could not take another step so the few who knew the danger that the night might bring yielded to the many, and we camped within three miles of the summit. That night came the dreaded snow. Around the campfires under the trees great feathery flakes came whirling down. The air was so full of them that one could see objects only a few feet away. . . . We children slept soundly on our cold bed of snow with a soft white mantle falling over us so quickly that every few moments my mother would have to shake the shawl—our only covering—to keep us from being buried alive. In the morning the snow lay deep on mountain and valley. With heavy hearts we turned back to a cabin that had been built by the Murphy-Schallenberger party two years before.

—*Virginia Reed, age 12*

Some of the party built tents out of the canvas from their wagons. Others built cabins. The Donner brothers built their camp six or seven miles east of the other settlers. By the middle of December, the group had killed and eaten all the cattle, and one man had died. They began eating bark, twigs, and boiled cowhides.

Since they were starving, a group of 17 started out on December 16 to try to get over the mountains to get help. Two came back and only seven, two men and five women, made it to an Indian camp. The other eight died on the way. It took them 32 days.

Meanwhile, many of those at the camps starved to death during that cold winter. Some survived by eating the flesh of those who had died. On February 19, 1847, the first rescue party arrived. They had been sent from Sutter's Fort, which was now about 150 miles away. John P. Rhoads and Resin P. Tucker led the 14-man party. They took some of the survivors to Johnson's Ranch, the first settlement they reached when they entered California.

In February, a second group from the Donner Party tried to make it over the top of the mountains. They met a second relief party coming. The third relief party to make it to the camps found George Donner and his family. He was dying and could not be moved, and his wife refused to leave him. The children were rescued. Several others were too weak to travel and remained at the camp. The last relief party arrived on April 7. They found one survivor, Louis Keseberg. All the others had died.

Out of the 89 members of the Donner party, only 47 survived. The other 42 died from starvation or from the freezing weather when they tried to make it over the mountains.

Plains Indians on horses.

Injuries killed a number of pioneers. Children sometimes fell under the wagons and were run over and killed. Many people drowned while crossing streams. Broken bones, cuts, burns, and animal and snake bites were fairly common. Wagons sometimes overturned, and cattle could stampede. People were sometimes gored or kicked by animals. Women's long skirts sometimes dragged them under wagons or animals, and sometimes they caught fire in the campfire.

Illness caused many deaths. Among diseases, cholera claimed the most lives. The disease struck suddenly, spread quickly, and sometimes killed in a day. Cholera was a problem back east, too. Some people thought they could escape it by joining a wagon train. But some wagon trains lost half their members or more to the disease. In their diaries, pioneers estimated they saw from 2,000 to 5,000 graves of those who died from cholera on the journey.

Other diseases included diphtheria, typhoid fever, ague, tuberculosis, and smallpox. Dysentery, an infection of the digestive system, could not be treated, so many died from it. Some people got malaria from being bitten by an infected mosquito. Malaria causes sweats, fever, chills, and pains in the abdomen.

Most people didn't talk about it or write about it in their journals, but finding privacy to go to the bathroom was a problem. Usually the men went one way and the women the other. Women could use their skirts to shield one another from view.

When people died, the funerals and burials were hurried. People sometimes took pictures of one another holding a dead child. A shallow grave was dug. In cold weather, it was easier to dig in the area where the campfire had been because it thawed the ground. Few people were buried in coffins. Most were wrapped in blankets or quilts, or even in hollowed-out logs. Most graves were not marked. The family usually tried to disguise the grave so their loved ones would not be dug up by animals or Indians.

The pioneers had a great fear of Indian attacks on the trail, which was one reason for putting the wagons in a circle. Often men took turns standing watch through the night. However, Indian attacks were actually quite rare, and fewer than 50 emigrants were killed by Indians.

Plains Indians

The Plains Indians included many tribes. The Sioux, Cheyenne, Arapaho, Blackfeet, Crow, Comanche, Pawnee, Shoshone, and Mandan were all Plains Indians. They lived in the central part of what is now the United States.

The Plains Indians lived by hunting, particularly buffalo. Most lived in buffalo-skin tepees with wooden poles. They often painted designs on them.

Most of their clothing was made from animal skins. The men wore leather leggings, a loincloth, and a belt. They usually didn't wear shirts. If they were cold, they wrapped a buffalo fur around their shoulders.

Women and girls wore dresses made from deerskin. Their jewelry was made from sea shells, metal, and beads. Clothing was often decorated with beadwork. The women also made moccasins for all the people of the tribe. They used buckskin and decorated them with quill work and beads.

The Plains Indians first saw horses around 1540, when Spanish explorers reached the Great Plains. The Spanish made a law that the Indians of the Southwest could not have horses. But those who worked on Spanish ranches learned to train horses and to ride them.

In 1680, the Indians revolted and drove the Spanish back into Mexico. Many of the horses were left behind, and the Indians began using them. By 1750, most of the Plains Indians had horses. That made it much easier to hunt buffalo. Also, a horse could pull a *travois*, which was made of sticks. It could carry loads of skins, tepees, and sometimes even people.

There were few conflicts in the early years between Europeans and Indians. The fur traders and Plains Indians got along and traded with each other. But when emigrants started going west by the thousands, the Plains Indians became alarmed. Some of them began harassing wagon trains and attacking pioneer settlements.

In the Treaty of 1851, the Plains Indians agreed to leave the wagon trains alone, in exchange for $50,000 a year. But the treaty wasn't very effective. When gold was discovered in Montana, prospectors swarmed through the Indians' best hunting grounds, and conflict followed. In 1868, another treaty was signed. The U.S. Army agreed to close down the Bozeman Trail (see page 39), and their forts along the trail.

(above) **Sioux woman in deerskin dress.**
Library of Congress LC-USZ62-110502

(left) **These Plains Indian tepees in Montana are decorated.**
Library of Congress LC-USZ62-101262

Sitting Bull

Dover Publications, Inc.

But that was not the end of the conflict. Miners flocked to the Black Hills when gold was discovered there in 1874. This was a sacred area to the Sioux Indians. Led by Sitting Bull and Crazy Horse, the Sioux fought the U.S. Army to protect the area. In 1876, U.S. Army lieutenant colonel George Armstrong Custer and his 250 soldiers were wiped out by the Sioux at the Battle of Little Bighorn.

The Nez Perce Indians, too, fought to keep their land, in the Wallowa Valley of northeastern Oregon. But in 1877, Chief Joseph and 1,700 of the Nez Perce surrendered to U.S. soldiers near the Canadian border.

The conflict between the settlers and the Indians finally ended in 1890 with the Wounded Knee Massacre in South Dakota (see page 112).

The Santa Fe Trail

Through the years, the pioneers heading west traveled on many different trails. The main ones included the Santa Fe Trail, the California Trail, the Oregon Trail, the Mormon Trail, and the

A Native American pulls a travois with his horse.

Library of Congress
LC-USZ62-97842

Bozeman Trail. Many of these trails ran together for many miles, and then divided in Wyoming or Utah.

In 1822, William Becknell took the first wagon train over the Santa Fe Trail. Because of this, he is known as the Father of the Santa Fe Trail. It started at Independence, Missouri, and ran to Santa Fe in what is now New Mexico.

He started out on August 4 from Missouri with three wagons and a number of other people. The wagons carried $3,000 in goods to sell in Santa Fe. Becknell followed the Arkansas River to about five miles west of where Dodge City, Kansas, now stands. Mountains lay ahead, and he knew he couldn't cross them with the wagons, so he headed south to the Cimarron River, about 50 miles away.

At one point, buffalo scared off the horses. Two men went to search for them and were attacked by Osage Indians who stole their guns, horses, and clothing. They had to cross the Cimarron Desert to reach the river, but the men ran out of water long before they got there. They were so thirsty they cut off their mules' ears and drank their blood. They arrived at the river just in time to keep from dying.

After that, the rest of the trip went smoothly. The group arrived in Santa Fe on November 16, where they sold their goods and made a $2,000 profit.

Traders used the Santa Fe Trail as a regular route from then until 1849. That year, when news spread of gold in California, thousands of gold seekers flooded the Santa Fe Trail.

ON THE TRAILS OF THE PIONEERS

What You Need

Crayons or markers
The map of the trails on page 34
Copy of the blank map

◄●►◄●►

You may want to draw the trails lightly in pencil first, then go over the pencil line with crayon or marker. Note: Some of your trails will overlap.

First, draw the Santa Fe Trail in red.
Then, draw the California Trail in blue.
Next, draw the Oregon Trail in green.
Draw the Mormon Trail in purple.
Finally, draw the Bozeman Trail in orange.

If you live west of the Mississippi River, mark your town on the map. If your ancestors traveled west, ask your parents where they came from in the East and mark that location as well. Otherwise, pick a location in the East that interests

you and mark that instead. Then figure out which trails the pioneers would have used to travel from that place to your town.

If you live east of the Mississippi, pick a place you'd like to live in the West. Mark it on your map. Then decide which trails you would have taken if you had moved there from the place where you live now.

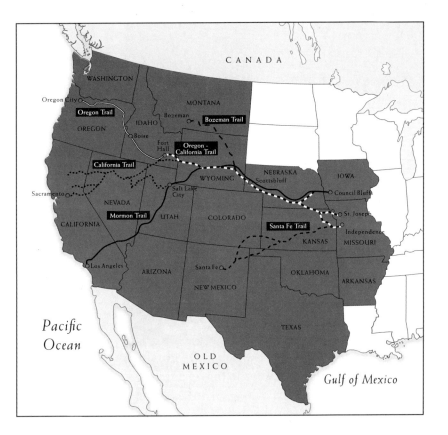

The main trails followed by pioneers moving west.

The California Trail

The California Trail had several starting places as well as several ending points. People started from various spots along the Missouri River. These short trails came together to follow the same path as the Oregon Trail. At different points in Nevada and Wyoming, the trail branched off toward destinations in different areas of California. One of these shortcuts, the Hastings Cut-Off, had proved disastrous for the Donner Party (see page 28).

In 1841, John Bidwell led the first group of emigrants across the California Trail. Three years later, Caleb Greenwood was the first to take wagons on the trail. During the Gold Rush in 1849–50, an estimated 70,000 gold-seekers crossed the country on the California Trail.

The Oregon Trail

The 2,170-mile Oregon Trail was the longest overland trail in North America. The first to cross the Oregon Trail in wagons were missionaries: Marcus and Narcissa Whitman, Henry and Eliza Spalding, and William H. Gray. They left St. Louis in the spring of 1836 and traveled much of the way with fur traders. They may not have realized it at the time, but Narcissa Whitman and Eliza Spalding were the first women of European ancestry to cross the Rocky Mountains.

About 1,000 people formed a wagon train at Independence, Missouri, in the spring of 1843. In what was called the Great Migration, they crossed the country on the Oregon Trail and reached the Oregon Country safely. The Oregon Country included the present states of Oregon and Washington, as well as part of Idaho.

Snow caps on the Sierra Nevadas. Donner Lake can be seen in the background.
Library of Congress LC-USZC4-11400

A JOURNAL ON YOUR TRIP WEST

Now that you've learned a lot about what it was like to go west with a wagon train, let's pretend you were one of the children whose parents moved west. Make a journal in which you can write about your trip.

What You Need

Ruler

Pencil

Scissors

Two pieces of lightweight cardboard, such
as tablet backs or poster board

2 sheets of print paper (this could be
wrapping paper or scrapbook paper)

White glue

2 sheets of plain paper

Paper punch

8 sheets of lined paper

Ribbon, 2 feet long

Measure and cut the cardboard so each piece is 5 inches by 8 inches. Cut the print paper so each piece is 8 inches by 10 inches. Lay one sheet of print paper on the table with the print side down. Cover one

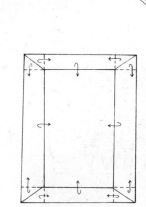

side of one of the pieces of cardboard with glue, lay it glue side down in the middle of the print paper, and press down. Cut from each corner of the paper to the corner of the cardboard.

Fold in the points on the corners, then fold each side in and glue them down.

Measure and cut the plain paper so it is 7½ by 9½ inches. Then glue it in the center, covering the cardboard.

Make the other cover the same way. Then, punch two holes in the long edge of each cover, about an inch from the top

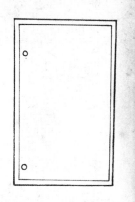

and bottom. Make sure the holes line up.

Measure and cut the lined paper so it is 7½ by 9½ inches. Punch holes in the lined paper to line up with the ones in the covers. Thread the ribbon through each hole from the back. Tie in a bow on the front. Trim off any extra.

Now you've made your journal! Imagine you're traveling along one of the western trails. Write at least three journal entries about your trip.

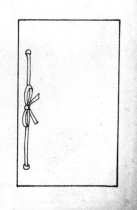

arcus Whitman was born in upstate New York, as was his wife, Narcissa Prentiss. He became a doctor and practiced in Canada for four years.

Narcissa was a very religious child. When she was 16, she pledged to become a missionary. The missionary board would not send an unmarried woman to the mission fields, so she finished her education and taught school. Henry Spalding, a fellow student, asked her to marry him. She turned him down.

While she was teaching, she met Marcus Whitman, who also wanted to be a missionary. They were married on February 16, 1836. The next day, they left for the Oregon Country, where they would be missionaries to the Native Americans.

Strangely enough, they traveled with her former suitor, Henry Spalding, and his wife, Eliza. Another missionary, William Gray, also went along. They traveled part of the way with fur traders and trappers. At first Marcus didn't relate well to them because of his refusal to drink alcohol. However, he won them over with his medical skills—he successfully removed an arrowhead from Jim Bridger's back (see page 17).

When they reached the Walla Walla Valley in September, the Whitmans decided to stay there and minister to the Cayuse Indians. After obtaining supplies at Fort Vancouver, the Spaldings moved farther east to Lapwai, near the present-day town of Lewiston, Idaho. There they worked with the Nez Perce Indians.

Narcissa gave birth to her only child, Alice Clarissa, on March 14, 1837. Narcissa adored her little daughter, but unfortunately, Alice drowned when she was two. Narcissa was depressed—she had no family or female friends to talk to—and her health suffered.

A Cayuse warrior.

Library of Congress LC-USZ62-89973

A year or so later, the Whitmans took in a young half-Indian girl named Helen Mar Meek. The next year, Jim Bridger left his half-Indian daughter, Mary Ann, in their care. Now Narcissa had children to care for, and that helped to fill the emptiness she had felt at the loss of Alice. Soon a little boy named David, who was half Indian and half Spanish, was taken into the household. Then Marcus's nephew, Perrin, joined the family.

Eventually they also took in the seven Sager children, two boys and five girls. Both their parents had died on the trip to Oregon.

Indian arrowheads

Photo by author, courtesy Garst Museum, Greenville, Ohio

So in a few years, Narcissa went from losing her only child to being the mother of 11!

At times, the Whitmans were discouraged at the lack of response from the Indians they were trying to convert. Several times Indians tried to intimidate them by forcing their way into their house and showing weapons.

The Cayuse became alarmed at the numbers of settlers moving onto their lands. A measles epidemic struck in 1847, affecting natives and settlers alike. Marcus Whitman gave medical aid to all, but most of the Indians died because they had no resistance to the disease. The Cayuse believed they weren't getting proper treatment and went on a rampage. They attacked the mission and killed the Whitmans and a dozen other people. A number of their children survived.

The survivors were held prisoner at the mission for a month. Then the Hudson Bay Company bought their freedom with blankets, shirts, beads, guns, and ammunition. The 46 survivors were taken to Oregon City, which was the capital of Oregon. Most of them found homes.

A group of 450 men who called themselves the Oregon Volunteers drove the Cayuse from the area. In 1859, six of the Cayuse were tried in Oregon City and found guilty of the murders. They were hanged.

By 1846, thousands of immigrants had crossed the country and settled in the Oregon Country. By 1868, over 50,000 people had moved west using the Oregon Trail.

The Mormon Trail

In 1846, the Mormons planned the best-organized mass migration in the history of the nation. On February 4, Brigham Young and 7,000 Mormons left Nauvoo, Illinois, and set out across Iowa. They left earlier than they had wanted to, because they were being persecuted, and planned to arrive at their destination before the winter of 1846–47.

They faced many hardships on their trip across Iowa. It was a bitterly cold winter.

A wagon train crosses the Rocky Mountains.

Library of Congress LC-DIG-pga-00894

Brigham Young
Dover Publications, Inc.

First wagons leave Nauvoo and cross the Mississippi River. The great severity of the weather and . . . the difficulty of crossing the river during many days of running ice, all combined to delay our departure, though for several days the bridge of ice across the Mississippi greatly facilitated the crossing.

—*Brigham Young, February 1846*

The Mormons were grouped in companies of 10, 50, and 100. They followed Native American trails and primitive roads across Iowa. Since they knew many others would follow them, they improved the trail as they went along. They even built camps along the way, planting crops and building shelters.

It took the first group four months to reach the Missouri River. A few settled along the river in Iowa and Nebraska. They built a camp called Winter Quarters near where Omaha, Nebraska, now stands.

About 4,000 people, including Young, spent the winter there. They resumed their westward trek on April 5, 1847. They followed the Platte and North Platte Rivers across the Great Plains for hundreds of miles. At Fort Laramie, they crossed the river and joined the Oregon Trail.

When they crossed the Continental Divide at South Pass, Horace Whitney wrote, "In advance of us, at great distance can be seen the outlines of mountains, loftier than any we have yet seen . . . their summits . . . covered with snow."

At Fort Bridger, they turned south and followed the trail the Donner Party had taken the year before. This was the most difficult 116 miles of the trip. By now most of them had walked 1,000 miles. Their wagons were worn out, and their livestock was weak. The trail led through narrow canyons filled with willows, over tree-covered hills, and over rocky ridges. It took the group 14 days to reach the Great Salt Lake Valley, arriving on July 24, 1847.

The Mormons wanted to establish a new state, called Deseret, with colonies from Canada to Mexico. Instead, the U.S. government in 1850 established a much smaller area around Salt Lake and called it Utah.

Mormon pioneers finally reach Salt Lake.
Library of Congress LC-USZ62-68162

The Bozeman Trail

In 1864, when gold was discovered in Colorado, the Bozeman Trail began as a shortcut to the gold fields. It was a short, decent wagon road with grass for the livestock to graze. But it was dangerous because it cut through the best hunting grounds of the Northern Plains Indians in the Powder River Basin.

About 3,500 people used the trail between 1863 and 1866. The Indians were furious, and this led to fighting between the military and the Indians. After five years of bloody battles, a peace treaty was signed by Red Cloud of the Sioux tribe. The trail was closed, forts abandoned, and the Powder River Basin was returned to the Sioux.

No matter how the pioneers traveled, the trip west was difficult, exhausting, and dangerous for those who made the trek. However, the trip itself was only the beginning of a new and different life for those who moved west.

➻ THE MORMON RELIGION ➻

The Mormon religion was founded by Joseph Smith. When he was 17 years old, he said he was visited by an angel named Moroni, who was the son of Mormon. Mormon, he said, was the leader of a tribe called the Nephites who had lived in the Americas.

According to Smith, Moroni told him he would be given gold plates containing the book of Mormon, which he would translate into English. Smith said he found the plates and Moroni helped him translate them. The book was published in 1830. During this time, Smith said John the Baptist appeared to him and ordained him to preach the true gospel, which he said had been lost from the earth.

People were upset with what they believed to be the false teachings of the Mormons. Some thought the Mormons worshipped many gods. Also, many were upset because the Mormons believed in *polygamy*, the practice of having more than one wife. Joseph Smith had 27 wives.

The group moved to Ohio, then to Missouri, then to Nauvoo, Illinois, to escape persecution. While in Nauvoo, Smith and his brother Hyrum were arrested for destroying a printing press. They claimed someone was printing harmful information about Mormonism. A mob later broke into the jail and killed the brothers.

The church then divided into two groups. One, led by one of Smith's widows, went back to Missouri. The other group, led by Brigham Young, went to Utah, where they founded Salt Lake City. Salt Lake City remains the center of the Mormon religion today. The church no longer practices polygamy.

Joseph Smith

Dover Publications, Inc.

3
Pioneer Homes

Most of the pioneers were on the trail for several months. During that time, they slept under the stars or in their wagons. When they finally reached their destination, the first thing they wanted to do was to build some type of home. Families often lived in their wagons until they finished building a more permanent home. Some built a lean-to out of brush and lived in it while they were building a house. Others slept in tents.

Before they could start building, they had to choose a good spot for their house. Water was scarce on the prairie, so they often tried to build their house near a stream or a spring. All water had to be carried to the house.

Pioneers might live in a dugout, a sod house, a log cabin, or a tarpaper shack. The kind of house they built depended on where they settled and what materials were available. Most families considered their cabins temporary homes. Their goal was to build a nice frame house within a few years, after a sawmill was set up in the area. However, the early settlers on the plains found that there were few trees, so there was little wood available for building.

Dugouts

The easiest and cheapest house to build was a dugout. One man said he built his 14-foot-square dugout for a cost of $2.78. That included the cost of the window and materials to make a door.

To build a dugout, pioneers would dig into the side of a hill or a creek bank until they had a room at least 8 feet by 10 feet. In this way, only the front wall had to be built. This was usually made of blocks of sod, piled up like bricks. Then they built a door frame and put in a door. Sometimes they would put a window frame into the sod wall.

This is the kind of house where the Ingalls family lived in Laura Ingalls Wilder's book *On the Banks of Plum Creek*. Their house had oiled paper in the window frame, since glass was expensive and hard to get. A dugout house was usually a temporary home until something better could be built. However, some people stayed in one for years.

With the arrival of Mother the dugout became the home of their dreams. When [she] was all set for housekeeping there was the "four-hole cook-stove" in one corner, the table in the opposite corner. In the other end of the 12 x 14 room were two beds, one above the other, for the children; another for the parents. The chairs were slices of a large cottonwood tree trunk, each set with three legs. All the furniture was the handiwork of Mr. Thompson. The room was warm in winter and comfortably cool in summer.

—*Elizabeth Thompson, Wirt, Nebraska, 1872*

Some people weren't quite as pleased with their dugouts, though. Some said they were damp and dirty and attracted bugs and worse.

(left) **A cow stands above the roof of a dugout.**
Library of Congress
LC-USZ62-8276

(right) **A dugout home in North Dakota.**
Library of Congress
LC-USZ62-72473

(left) **A sod house on the Nebraska prairie.**
Library of Congress LC-USZ62-30383

(above) **A farmer with oxen plows up sod on the prairie.**
Library of Congress LC-USZ62-100542

Sometimes the bull snakes would get in the roof and now and then one would lose his hold and fall down on the bed, then off on the floor. Mother would grab the hoe and there was something doing and after the fight was over Mr. Bull Snake was dragged outside.

—Recollection of another early settler, date unknown

Soddies

Sod houses were a little more permanent. Soddies, as they were called, were built of blocks of sod. First the pioneers had to find grass with densely packed roots that would hold the sod together. Buffalo grass, little blue stem, wire grass, and Indian grass were some of the kinds they used.

It took about an acre of sod to build a house. They would mow the area first, so the grass would be short. If they were lucky, they owned a sod plow or grasshopper plow. When hitched to horses or oxen, the plow would turn up a strip of sod about a foot wide and three to six inches thick. The men used a sharp spade to cut the strip into foot-and-a-half lengths.

These would become the building blocks, which would be laid together like bricks. The foundation was laid by placing the strips grassy side down in the outline of the house. It was very important for this first layer to be level. Most pioneers used a double row of sod blocks, making the walls about two feet thick.

An adze was used to make the logs of a log house square.

Photo by author

Sometimes a fireplace of sod blocks would be built into one wall. The builder needed to find some wood to use as door and window frames. The frames were fastened to the walls with wooden pegs. The door sometimes had leather hinges. Often windows were bought already framed.

The hardest part of building a sod house was putting on the roof. Builders needed to put pieces of lumber or timber across the tops of the walls. Sometimes wood from the wagons was used for the doors, window frames, and roof.

The slope of the roof was important, too. If it was too steep, the strips of sod slid or eroded off. But if it wasn't steep enough, water wouldn't run off when it rained hard. After the wooden part of the roof was built, it was covered with blocks of sod. On the roof, it was placed grassy side up, and in the summer, flowers sometimes grew on it.

The inner walls were smoothed with an axe, and then often plastered with a mixture of clay and ashes. Sometimes they were whitewashed, which made the room lighter and more cheerful. Some people papered the walls with newspapers to help insulate them. The floor was usually dirt, but as soon as possible, they tried to get enough lumber to lay a board floor over it.

Most sod houses had only one room. Sometimes the family would hang a sheet or coverlet up to divide the sleeping quarters from the rest of the house.

These houses were cool in summer and warm in winter. However, they were sometimes damp, and when it rained hard, the roof usually leaked. One man said, "It rained two days longer inside than it did outside."

The small house in which I was born had dirt walls, a dirt floor and a dirt roof. . . . It was cool and nice except when it rained. . . . If this roof sprang a leak, it was just too bad. First there would be a drop or two of water. Then the hole would widen—a fine example of erosion—and Mother would grab buckets, tubs, dishpans, anything to catch the muddy stream.

—*Edith Kitt, Arizona, remembering in 1964*

Log Cabins and Log Houses

Many of the earlier pioneers built log cabins or log houses. In areas like Ohio, Indiana, Illinois, and Wisconsin, there was plenty of wood available. In fact, the trees were quite a hindrance because an area had to be cleared before a cabin could be built. Also, the pioneers had to clear large areas for farming.

Log cabins are not the same as log houses. Log cabins were usually built with round logs that had most of the bark left on.

When building a log house, settlers usually made the logs square by cutting off the rounded part with an *adze*. This was a tool that looked somewhat like a hammer with a sharp blade instead of a flat surface to pound with.

Early houses faced south, which kept the cold north winds from blowing in and also let more light in the door and window. Pioneers could tell time by checking to see how far into the room the sunlight came.

Logs were usually a little bigger on one end than the other, because trees are wider at the bottom than at the top. For that reason, one log would be laid with the big end on one side, and the next with the big end on the other side. The builder made a notch on the top of each end of the log, then fitted the logs together at the corners using the notches. It took skill to cut them just right so they would fit together. If you've ever played with Lincoln Logs, you will understand how the notches fit together.

When the walls were about six or seven logs high, two people could no longer lift the logs to the top. Sometimes one builder was stationed on top of the wall and others would lean two logs against the wall with their tops on top of the wall. Two people would roll a log up these logs, while the person at the top pulled on a rope tied around the middle of the log. In this way they were able to get heavy logs up higher.

After the walls were built, holes were cut for a door and windows. The hinges on the door were often made from wood or leather, but later iron hinges were used. The door usually opened out so it didn't take up room in the cabin. Inside the door was a wooden latch and crossbar to lock the door. Sometimes a leather strap called a *latchstring* would be connected to the latch and run through a hole in the door. If you pulled on the latchstring from outside, it would lift the latch and open the door.

The windows often didn't have glass. Some were covered with oiled paper to let light in and keep out rain. And sometimes animal skins were hung over the windows in winter to keep out the cold.

Often several pioneers got together to help build a cabin. This was called a *cabin raising* or *house raising*. They would build the walls and lay timbers for the roof. Then they laid handmade shingles in overlapping rows so water would drain off the top of the cabin. These shingles were split with a tool called a *froe*. They were much larger than present-day shingles, three to four feet long.

After the neighbors left, the family still had lots to do. They needed to build a stone fireplace and a chimney. Some chimneys were made of stone, and others were made from sticks and mud. They also needed to chink between the logs. Even the best cut and fitted logs had spaces between them where wind, snow, and rain could blow in. To stop this, sometimes small pieces of wood and stones were wedged between the logs. Then they were sealed with moss or wet clay that was sometimes mixed with animal hair or straw. This was called *chinking*.

Most log cabins were just one room. The length of the longest wall was limited by the height of the

An old log cabin built with round logs.

Library of Congress LC-DIG-ppmsc-02164

trees available and the amount of weight one or two people could lift in putting the logs in place.

Some people built what was called a "dog-trot" cabin. This was really two cabins set next to each other. They built a roof over the space between the two cabins, making kind of a covered porch called a dog-trot. Others built a one-room cabin, and then attached a lean-to to one side to use for a kitchen.

The floors were often dirt, which was soon packed hard by the feet of everyone in the family. Sometimes builders split logs in half and laid them flat-side-up for a floor. This was called a *puncheon floor*.

Often, if the roof was high enough, families would build a loft above the main room of the cabin. This provided a place for children to sleep. To get to the loft, kids had to climb a wooden ladder or pegs hammered into the wall.

A log house typical of one people would build after they had been settled for several years.

Photo by author, courtesy Darke County Parks, Darke County, Ohio

BUILD A LOG CABIN

Here's a little log cabin you can build with materials that are easy to find.

What You Need

Half-pint milk carton
Scissors
Tape
Brown paper, from grocery bag
Glue
Craft knife
Dinner knife
Peanut Butter
Pretzel sticks
Corrugated cardboard, from a box
Pen or marker

Wash out a half-pint milk carton and dry it. Cut off the top flap, then tape the top shut. Cut a door out of brown paper and glue in the center of the front of the carton.

Cut around three sides of the door so it will open. You might want to get an adult to help you do this with a craft knife. Have an adult use the same craft knife to cut a window in one side of the carton.

Use a dinner knife to spread peanut butter on the front of the carton. Break off a pretzel stick to fit the carton and stick it to one corner of the front, going up and down. One by one, break off pieces of pretzel to fit between the door and the sides. (Biting is the easiest way to get them the right size!) Put a final pretzel above the door.

Spread peanut butter on the other three sides, one at a time, and cover with pretzels. You may need two vertical pretzels on some corners.

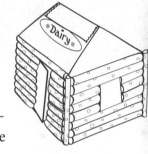

Cut a piece of corrugated cardboard into a rectangle 3 inches by 4½ inches. Make sure the corrugations (grooves) are running across the short side. Bend the cardboard in the center to make a roof. Before you glue the roof on, use a marker or pen to draw shingles.

(above) **Woman cooking.**

Photo by author, courtesy Darke County Parks, Greenville, Ohio

(right) **Washstand**

Courtesy Laura James

Life at Home as a Pioneer

Some settlers had only furniture they made themselves. Others had a few treasured items brought from back east. Most families had several children, so there wasn't room in a one-room cabin for a lot of furniture. A table, a few chairs, and beds might be the only furnishings. Often several children slept in one bed. Wooden pegs were inserted in the walls to hang clothing, utensils, and other things.

Usually the fireplace was used for both heating and cooking. A few pioneers had stoves, but most new arrivals cooked in the fireplace. A good deal of heat escaped up the chimney when it was windy.

Matches were very rare in the early days. Fire had to be made by using flint and steel to get a spark, or using the *bow and drill* method. In this method, a pioneer spun a long, smooth stick of hard wood between his hands with the tip boring into a piece of soft, dry wood. Eventually, the friction would cause the soft wood to catch fire. People tried to never let their fires go out. If it did, they usually went to the neighbors and borrowed some hot coals from them to get their own fires started again.

> I was about grown before I ever saw a match for starting fires. If we got out of fire at home, we would have to go to a neighbor and borrow fire.
>
> —*Mary Whisner, mid-1840s*

During nice weather, a lot of the work could be done outside. One chore often done outdoors was the laundry. It could take all day. A large washtub was filled with several buckets of water carried from the spring or a nearby stream. A fire was built under the tub to heat the water, and homemade soap was added. The washer then scrubbed the clothes on a washboard. With that done, the laundry had to be rinsed with clean water, and because pioneers didn't have clotheslines, clothes were often draped over fences or bushes, or laid on the ground to dry.

None of these houses had indoor plumbing, which meant all the water had to be carried from the nearest stream or spring. And water was needed for cooking, drinking, bathing, and doing laundry. Getting water was often the job of the children. It was usually an uphill trip back to the house with the full bucket of water.

Of course, there were no bathrooms. Families built outhouses to use as their toilets. An outhouse was located fairly close to the house because the settlers might have to use it at night or during cold weather. They didn't want it too close, though, because it didn't always smell good.

To construct an outhouse, the builder first dug a deep pit. Then a small building was built above the hole. An opening, often a half-moon shape, was cut into the door of the outhouse. This let in a little fresh air without letting in rain and snow. A wooden bench was built across the building, above the pit, with one or two holes, where they would sit. Sometimes they sprinkled lime in the hole to reduce the smell. Imagine how it might smell if you never flushed! Toilet paper hadn't been invented, so pioneers used pages from catalogs, or even cornhusks.

When it was time to bathe, usually not more than once a week, a big washtub was brought in the house. Buckets of water were heated, and then poured into the tub. Then the family bathed, one at a time, in the same water.

Dinner Time

Pioneers spent most of their time obtaining and preparing food. Of course, there were no grocery stores at first. Pioneers hunted meat for their families—deer, squirrels, turkeys, and rabbits. Wild pigs were plentiful, too, so most families ate a lot of pork.

With no refrigerators or freezers, the pioneers had to use other methods to preserve their meat. When they first shot a deer or buffalo, they ate some of the fresh meat. Meat that would be eaten within a few days could be par-boiled, or partly cooked. That would preserve it for a few days, and then they would finish cooking it. Most of the meat, though, had to be preserved for later.

A number of other foods settlers ate came from nature. They were often able to find blackberries, huckleberries, and chokecherries. Settlers had to be on the lookout for bears while they were picking, because bears love berries, too. Sometimes they found plums. Both plums and berries could be made into jams and jellies. Honey and maple syrup also came from natural sources. Watercress grew along streams and provided a fresh vegetable for salad.

Many pioneers had a cow for milk, or bought milk from neighbors who did. Some raised a cow for beef, so they had fresh meat once a year when they butchered. Some families also raised chickens, which provided them with eggs and an occasional chicken dinner. They could also sell the extra eggs to neighbors who didn't have their own chickens.

(top) **Pioneers used washtubs and washboards.**

Photo by author, courtesy Garst Museum, Greenville, Ohio

(bottom) **A mother bathes her child in a tub.**

Library of Congress LC-USZ62-85874

49

PRESERVING
⫸ MEAT ⫷

There were several methods pioneers used to preserve meat. Some of it was smoked. They would build a fire, let it burn down to hot coals, then put green wood on top of the coals. This caused a lot of smoke. Strips of meat would be hung just above the fire, and the smoke would preserve it.

Beef jerky was made by cutting beef into long, narrow strips. Pioneers salted the strips, hung them on a wooden rack in the sun, and left them there till the meat was hard. It usually took two or three days.

Some meat, particularly pork, was pickled. First, the meat would be packed into barrels. Then the barrels would be filled with brine—water with lots of salt—with a little sugar and saltpeter added. The meat had to be left in the brine for three days for each pound of meat, and the brine had to be changed now and then to be sure it didn't sour.

Woman milking cow.
Library of Congress LC-USZ62-112640

Early settlers did have to buy a few things, including tea, vinegar, salt, coffee, flour, sorghum, and spices. If they couldn't get maple syrup or honey, they sometimes bought a little sugar, but it was expensive.

As soon as they found a place to live, the family would start plowing the land to plant a garden. On the prairie, it was difficult to plow because of the dense, tangled roots. Often it took a full day to plow one acre. However, it was even more difficult to prepare the land for planting if the settlers lived on forested land. Trees had to be cut and stumps removed if possible.

Pioneers planted many food crops, most of them vegetables. These included corn, beets, turnips, beans, onions, carrots, squash, peas, pumpkins, and potatoes. Some also planted buckwheat and apple trees.

Apples were very useful. They could be dried or eaten fresh. They could be used to make apple fritters, apple cobbler, applesauce, apple pie, and fried apples. Apples were even used as the faces for children's dolls!

The pioneers also made apple butter. This was made outside in a huge kettle over an open fire. The apples were peeled and cored, then put into the kettle with apple cider. They were cooked all day, with someone stirring the mixture all the time. Then the apple butter was put into tightly capped jars.

Fruits and vegetables were eaten fresh all summer, but the pioneers had to find ways to preserve them to eat during the winter. It was important to eat these foods all year to prevent scurvy. The disease is caused by a lack of vitamin C and can cause spongy gums, tooth loss, and spots on the arms and legs. It causes people to feel tired and weak. Pioneers understood this and took care to keep fruits and vegetables in their diet all year round.

Many of the fruits settlers ate were dried. To dry the fruit, they spread it out, covered it with cheesecloth, and left it in the sun until it shriveled up and got hard. When they were ready to eat it, they soaked it in water, and then stewed it with sugar to make it taste better. Some of the fruit was also made into jam or jelly.

Vegetables were stored in a *root cellar*. To make a root cellar, a room was dug in the side of a hillside or underground, and a wooden door was built. The root cellar would keep vegetables such

LOG CABIN DIORAMA

You have read about log cabins and the way they were furnished. You've made a little cabin with pretzels. Now let's think about the inside of the cabin.

What You Need

Shoebox
Brown paper, from a grocery bag
White glue or glue stick
Crayons or markers
Scissors
Pebbles

You don't need the lid of the shoebox. Cover the outside on three sides and the bottom with brown paper and glue it down. Lay the box on its side and draw logs with a brown crayon or marker. (If you want, use pretzels for logs like you did in Build a Log Cabin on page 47.)

With the box in its side, you're looking into the cabin through the opening in the front wall. Remember, most log cabins were one room. Cut a window in the back. You may need to poke a hole in the middle of the window first, before you use your scissors. You don't need a door, because your cabin is open in the front.

Draw a fireplace in back. Glue pebbles to cover the fireplace. Be sure to leave an opening to cook.

Color the floor brown. If you want a dirt floor, it's done. If you want a puncheon floor, draw the logs. (If you want to be more realistic, use popsicle sticks for the puncheon floor.)

Fill the cabin with items pioneers owned, but remember, they didn't own much. Make beds, a table, and stools, benches, or chairs.

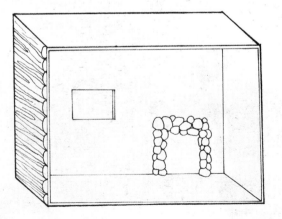

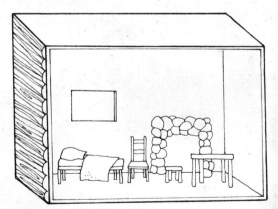

51

as potatoes, onions, carrots, turnips, pumpkins, and beets fresh. It kept them cool in summer, and the earth insulated the root cellar in winter, so the food didn't freeze.

If a family had a spring on their property, they would build a *springhouse*. Since they didn't have refrigerators, this helped them keep foods like milk, butter, cheese, and eggs fresh. Usually a small stone house was built over the spring, which was ice cold. The food was put in ceramic crocks, which were placed in the spring. The water stayed at the same temperature all year round, keeping the food cool.

Much of the corn the pioneers grew was shelled, usually by the children. Some of it was fed to the livestock, but much of it was ground into cornmeal. Most of the bread the early settlers ate was cornbread.

After a pioneer family had been settled for a while, they might be lucky enough to get a stove. In the meantime, they made the best of cooking in a fireplace.

A metal arm or bracket was usually built into the fireplace to hold a large cast-iron kettle. Some kettles had legs so they could set in the fire. These were called *spiders*. Another important kind of utensil was the Dutch oven. It was a heavy iron kettle with a lid. The food was put in the kettle, which was then set in the coals. More hot coals were piled on top of the lid so that the food cooked from both the bottom and the top.

Butter was made in a large wooden churn. First, cream was poured into the churn, then

(left) **Springhouse**
Library of Congress LC-DIG-mpcc-00166

(right) **Little girl with apple.**
Library of Congress LC-USZ62-5982

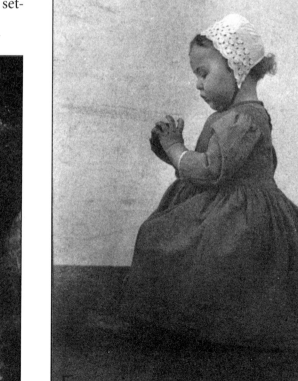

52

APPLE BUTTER

You can make an easy version of apple butter in your microwave without having to spend all day stirring a mixture of apples in a huge kettle.

What You Need

4 medium apples
Knife
½ cup apple juice
Large glass bowl
Spoon
Blender
½ cup sugar
½ teaspoon cinnamon
¼ teaspoon pumpkin pie spice
Jars to put your apple butter in

Cut each apple in four pieces and cut out the core, but leave the skin on. Put the apples and juice in the bowl.

Place the bowl in a microwave on high for 9 minutes. Stop every three minutes and stir. The skins should become loose during cooking.

Once it has cooled, take out the skins. Pour the rest of the mixture into a blender and blend until smooth.

Put the mixture back in the bowl. Add sugar, cinnamon, and pumpkin pie spice.

Microwave on high for 10 minutes, or until thick.

Put in jars and keep in the refrigerator. When you're ready to eat, try spreading apple butter on your cornbread (see page 54).

CORNBREAD

You can make cornbread like the pioneers did, but to make it a little easier you can use an oven instead of a fireplace.

What You Need

Measuring cups
Measuring spoons
1 cup cornmeal
1 teaspoon baking soda
1 teaspoon salt
Large bowl
Big spoon
¼ cup butter or margarine to melt
Small bowl
1 cup milk
2 eggs
Another tablespoon of butter
Iron skillet

Turn the oven on and set it for 450 degrees. Put the cornmeal, baking soda, and salt in a large bowl and mix.

Melt ¼ cup butter in the microwave in a small bowl. Measure the milk, then add it to the melted butter. Add milk and butter mixture to the big bowl and stir. Finally, add two eggs and stir well.

Put the tablespoon of butter in an iron skillet and put in the oven for three minutes. Use an oven mitt to remove the skillet from the oven. It will be very hot. Set it on top of the stove.

Pour the batter into the skillet. Use the oven mitt to put the skillet back in the oven.

Bake until golden brown, about 25 minutes. When done, allow it to cool before eating.

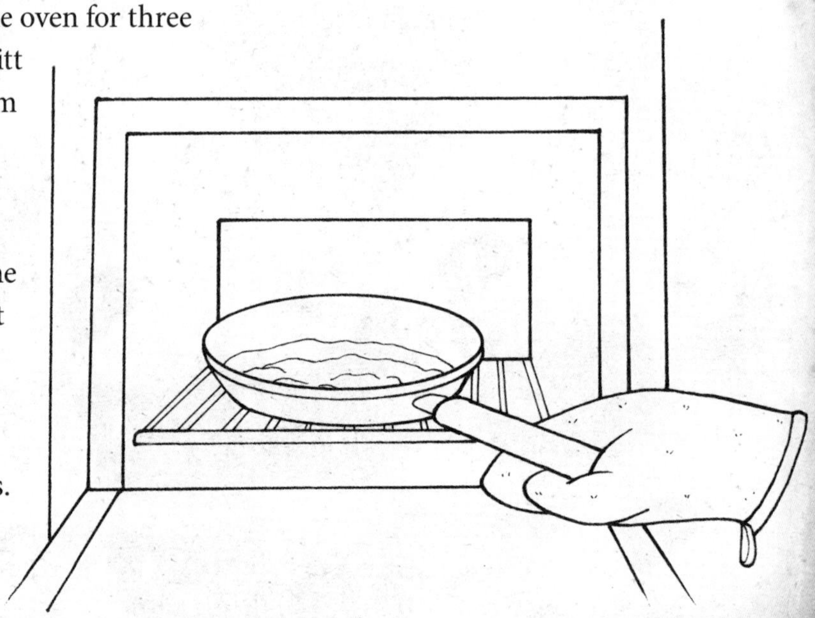

covered with a lid that had a hole in the center. A wide wooden paddle called a *dasher* fit inside the churn and a handle, similar to a broomstick, extended from the top of lid. The dasher was pounded up and down until butter formed. This took a long time and was usually the job of the young girls in the family. Sometimes they sang or made up rhymes to keep the rhythm going. When the butter finally formed, they lifted it out of the churn and put it in a wooden bowl, then rinsed it several times to get it clean. They added a little salt, and sometimes they put the butter into a pretty mold. The buttermilk left in the churn was good to drink.

Since some foods were hard to come by, pioneers became adept at substituting ingredients they had for the ones they couldn't get. Instead of lemons or lemon juice, they used vinegar. Wild chicory was used as a coffee substitute. And they sweetened their food with honey, molasses, or maple syrup when they didn't have sugar.

Life in a pioneer home was not only harder than our lives today, but it was also more difficult that the lives most of the pioneers had known back home.

Dutch oven
Photo by author, courtesy Darke County Parks, Greenville, Ohio

4
Community Life

Most pioneers who settled in the West were farmers. After the Homestead Act of 1862 went into effect, a large number of them went west to get free land. In order to claim land, the settler had to file a claim at the nearest land office. The homesteader was required to improve the land, including building a house. He had to live in the house for five years, and then he could file for a deed. Anyone who had never "taken up arms," or fought, against the U.S. government was allowed to file for a homestead. This included freed slaves.

Pioneer Towns

Although most settlers in the West lived on farms, small towns grew up in all areas. At first pioneers had to be mostly self-sufficient, but after a while, they usually had a little extra cash and were able to buy some things in town. They didn't go to town often, but when they did, they bought things they could not make at home or grow on their farms.

When people started moving west and settling in large numbers, storekeepers and other people who provided services saw an opportunity to make money. They built businesses and homes in small clusters near groups of homesteaders and other settlers. Some skilled laborers also moved to these towns to provide services such as blacksmithing.

Inns or hotels were opened and needed workers. General stores, gristmills, sawmills, and other

The Colorado settlement of Black Hawk Point in 1862.
Library of Congress
LC-DIG-ppmsca-09931

buildings were added to the towns. The people who ran them built houses in town.

When there were a number of young children in the area, a school was usually built, and that required a teacher to move to town. Church was often held in the school until a separate church building could be built.

Then ministers lived in town, unless they were *circuit riders*. The circuit riders traveled by horseback and preached at each of several churches in turn. A church might only have a preacher once every six weeks. Because they rode on horseback they were sometimes known as *saddlebag preachers*. Circuit riders carried with them only what they could carry in the saddlebags on either side of the horse. The Methodist faith was the first denomination to have circuit riders.

Most small towns had a general store. It sold many different items, since there were not separate grocery stores, clothing stores, department stores, and other businesses like we have now. The post office was often located in the general store.

There was usually a land title office, where people could file their claims for homesteads. They also got their title deeds there after they had lived on their claims for five years.

The blacksmith shop was an important business. The biggest business for the blacksmith was making horseshoes and fitting them on horses. Blacksmiths also repaired broken metal tools and implements. They could make new *plowshares* (blades) and wagon parts. A harness shop repaired and sold harnesses, saddles, and boots.

Most towns had a livery stable. Here a person could rent a horse and buggy. People could also

BLACK SETTLERS

Following the Civil War, many African Americans moved west. It was a way to escape their poor treatment in the South. The Ku Klux Klan, an organization that believed whites were superior to blacks, made the former slaves' lives miserable. The Klan was responsible for many acts of violence against blacks.

After the slaves were freed, most kept working on the plantations of the South because they had no money to buy land or start businesses. But the Homestead Act of 1862 was a way for them to get land. Black settlers from Georgia, Alabama, Mississippi, Tennessee, Louisiana, and Alabama streamed westward.

Those who weren't homesteaders got jobs. Some worked as cattle drivers, teachers, railroad workers, nurses, or fur traders. Others cleaned, cooked, made clothes, or worked in a mine.

In many places, African Americans started their own all-black towns. Here they were free to own land, open businesses, and govern themselves. They could live in peace and escape much of the prejudice and poor treatment they had known.

Langston, Oklahoma, was one of these towns. Edwin P. McCabe, an African American, had served two terms as state auditor in Kansas. When Oklahoma was opened to settlers in 1890, he bought 320 acres of land and started a town for blacks. It was named for John M. Langston, who was the first black Congressman from Virginia. McCabe set aside 40 acres for a college to be built. The Oklahoma Colored Agricultural and Normal University trained people in farming and teaching.

The community of Longtown, in western Ohio, has a different sort of history. It was founded by free blacks, but settlers included blacks, whites, and Native Americans. James Clemens, a free-born African American, was the first settler in Longtown in 1818. Over the years, many freed slaves settled there. In 1845 a well-known vocational school, the Union Literary Institute, opened in Longtown. One of its students, Hiram Rhodes Revels, became the first black U.S. senator in 1870.

At its peak, Longtown had nearly 900 residents. It had two churches, a school, and other community buildings. In the 1950s and '60s, the Longtown softball team was well-known in the area and chalked up many victories. Today there are only 10 families left, although many other people in the surrounding area trace their roots back to Longtown. One church is still open.

A sod house in the black community of Bracketville, Texas.

Library of Congress
LC-USZ62-125338

keep their horses there if they didn't have a place for them at home. People staying at the inn often boarded their horses at the livery stable.

As towns grew, so did the businesses and services in them. Sometimes a resident would open a print shop and start a newspaper, which would usually come out once a week. Most towns had a

Sutler's General Store in Fort Dodge, Kansas.
Library of Congress LC-USZ62-116768

A blacksmith at work in his shop.
Library of Congress LC-USZ62-101317

doctor after they became established, and some had a dentist, as well. Banks and barber shops opened in many towns, and there were even some dress shops.

Walnut Grove, Minnesota

Walnut Grove, Minnesota, was a typical pioneer small town in the mid-1800s. It was established in 1870 and was named for a beautiful grove of walnut trees along Plum Creek, just outside of town. Many homesteaders had settled along Plum Creek, so the town grew up nearby.

Today, Walnut Grove is located in southeast Minnesota on Highway 14. That road is also called the Laura Ingalls Wilder Historic Highway because Laura lived in Walnut Grove for a few years. The Ingalls family left Walnut Grove after grasshoppers wiped out their crops two years in a row.

The town grew quickly. The first postmaster of Walnut Grove, Elias Bedal, also taught children in his home starting in 1873. The Congregational Church was built the next year. About this time, there were three general stores in Walnut Grove, a hardware store, drug store, grocery store, flour mill, feed store, harness shop, blacksmith shop, doctor's office, law office, and saloon.

The land was rich and the hunting was good, and more and more people settled in the area. Walnut Grove grew and did well until 1873, when the grasshopper plague began. That caused many people to leave the area as their crops were all ruined.

Things slowly improved after the plague was over in 1877. The Ingalls family moved back to town. In 1879, Walnut Grove was incorporated. Charles Ingalls, Laura's father, served as the first justice of the peace.

Walnut Grove has grown through the years, but it's still a small town. The town is one square mile in size and in the last census reported about 600 people. There are 40 businesses in town and six churches. Walnut Grove has two schools, an elementary and a middle school. High school students from Walnut Grove attend the high school in nearby Westbrook.

Just outside of town is the Plum Creek County Park. This park has a campground, a hiking trail, ballfields, picnic shelter, and sledding in winter. In summer, people enjoy swimming and fishing in Lake Laura. The Laura Ingalls Wilder Museum in town consists of seven buildings. They include a little red schoolhouse, a typical pioneer home, a chapel, an 1898 depot, and a covered wagon display.

Lawrence, Kansas

Lawrence, Kansas, was a different type of frontier town. Unlike Walnut Grove, it was planned. The New England Emigrant Society of Massachusetts sent two men to choose a place in Kansas for an antislavery settlement. The society's purpose was to help people migrate to Kansas. Nearby Missouri was a slave state, and the people there hoped that Kansas would be a slave state, too. The New England Emigrant Society had other ideas.

The town was founded in 1854. It had several names. First it was Wakarusa, then Yankeetown, Excelsior, and New Boston. It was finally named Lawrence for Amos Adams Lawrence, an abolitionist politician.

⫸ THE GRASSHOPPER PLAGUE ⫷

From 1874 to 1876, hordes of grasshoppers swarmed over much of the Great Plains. They were actually Rocky Mountain locusts, rather than grasshoppers, but they looked a lot like grasshoppers, so that's what most people called them. Whenever they landed, they ate everything in sight. Many farmers found all their crops destroyed.

Green grasshoppers of all sizes were swarming everywhere and eating. The wind could not blow loud enough to hide the sound of their jaws, nipping, gnawing, chewing. They ate all the green garden rows. They ate the green potato tops. They ate the grass, and the willow leaves, and the green plum thickets and the small green plums. They ate the whole prairie bare and brown. Thick over all the ground they were hopping, and Laura and Mary stayed in the house.

—*Laura Ingalls Wilder* in
On the Banks of Plum Creek

The worst thing was that the grasshoppers had laid eggs in the ground. The next summer they hatched. Again, the grasshoppers swarmed over the land and devoured the crops.

Grasshoppers made their appearance in this county again on the 2d of October. The wind was blowing them from the southwest during the day . . . the sky was darkened with them. They soon covered the entire county, and at once began their onslaught upon the wheat fields. . . . In a few days, scarcely a spear of wheat was to be seen over the entire county.

—*Joseph Tilden,*
Carthage, Missouri, 1876

A humorous picture of a man watching the grasshoppers arrive was on a stereograph card. The stereograph was something like the View-Masters we have now.

Library of Congress LC-DIG-ppmsca-09649

ADVERTISE FREE LAND IN THE WEST

Imagine you're in charge of making a poster for the government to use to advertise land available through the Homestead Act.

What You Need

Poster board
Markers or crayons

●➤●➤

Decide how to make your poster get someone's attention and make him or her want to homestead. It could be bright colors, large lettering, or an interesting picture. Make sure the title is large and easy to read. Be sure to include pictures.

Put the most important information about the Homestead Act on the advertisement, and tell its readers where they can get more information.

WHO AM I?

Now that you've read all about different jobs people did in early communities, you can play this game. This is best for a fairly large group.

What You Need

Index cards
Pen or pencil
Pins or tape

●➤●➤

Before you begin, write on each card the name of a job people did in pioneer days.

To start, place the cards face down in a pile. Have someone who's not playing pin or tape a card on each person's back. Now everyone but you can see what your job is.

Go around asking people questions about your job that can be answered by yes or no. The game ends when everyone has figured out what his or her pioneer job is.

The first group of 29 emigrants traveled up the Missouri River from St. Louis to Kansas City. They walked the last 40 miles to the site of the new town of Lawrence. Ox teams carried their baggage and belongings. When they arrived at the site, they pitched 25 tents on Mount Oread. At first, they voted in favor of building the town there, but a few days later they decided to move it closer to the Kansas River.

A larger group of 67 people, including eight or 10 women and several children, left Boston in August. They arrived at the site in September. Many of the men in the group became well known in Kansas history. For instance, Charles Robinson was the first governor of Kansas, and Samuel C. Pomeroy became one of the state's first senators.

On September 20 the two groups met and laid out the town. They agreed upon some rules and elected officers for the city government. The town council prohibited the sale of alcoholic beverages for anything but "medicinal, mechanical, or manufacturing purposes." This made Lawrence a "dry" town, as alcohol-free communities were called.

> **A few tents were pitched on high ground overlooking the Kansas and Wakarusa valleys; others were scattered over the level bottom lands below, but not a dwelling besides could be seen. It was a city of tents alone.**
>
> —*Rev. Charles B. Boyington, c. 1854*

The settlers then set to work building the town. The first house was a 14-foot-square log cabin close to the river. Lumber wasn't plenti-

Cattle grazing on Mount Oread, near Lawrence, Kansas.
Library of Congress LC-DIG-stereo-00166

ful, so many people built what was called a *hay tent*. They set up two rows of poles, touching at the top. Then they thatched the sides with hay from the prairie. The other two sides were built up with sod blocks.

Rev. S. Y. Lum preached the first sermon in the new town in a boarding house built in this style. They used some trunks for a pulpit and the beds and boxes of the boarders for seats. That was the birth of the Plymouth Congregational Church. It was the first church in Kansas with the exception of the missionaries' churches.

> **Last Sabbath . . . was the first Sabbath our parties had assembled for the "hearing of the word." Rev. Mr. Lum, sent us by the American Home Missionary**

Society, preached very acceptably. The place of the meeting was one of the large receiving and boarding houses . . . very warm and very good. We had a large and attentive audience.

—An attendee at that first service, in a letter home, 1854

The first Lawrence school opened in 1855. The people paid for it by contributions, and all students were welcome. Mr. E. P. Fitch was the first teacher.

Two newspapers can lay claim to being the first in Lawrence. The first issue of the *Kansas Tribune* was printed in Medina, Ohio, on October 15, 1854 and then taken to Lawrence to be distributed. The first paper actually printed in Lawrence was the *Kansas Free State*. Its first issue was dated January 3, 1855. It stated it was published from an office that had neither "floor, ceiling, nor window sash."

The settlers were lucky that their first winter was a mild one. There was a big snowstorm on November 12, 1854, but it soon passed, and the weather warmed up. At Christmas it was so warm that people had their windows open and were sitting outside. There was another cold spell late in January, but on the whole, it was a very warm winter.

Also in 1854, a problem arose when hundreds of people from Missouri crossed the border into Kansas and marked off land. They drove in stakes with their names on them, then left. They did this to prevent more free-state supporters from moving to Kansas. The Missourians weren't following the law, so their claims weren't legal. But when new settlers came, they couldn't find any land near Lawrence that wasn't already claimed. Eventually, after several confrontations and threats, the Missourians left. However, they continued to hassle the free-staters from time to time.

Because the people who lived there were anti-slavery, Lawrence served as an important stop on the Underground Railroad. Many escaped slaves were helped to freedom by the people of the town.

Lawrence even became the headquarters of the Free State Party. The party was determined that Kansas would be a free state. The nearby Missourians wanted it to be a slave state, and trouble began again. In May 1856, they looted the town and burned down the Free-State Hotel.

After the Civil War, Lawrence prospered and continued to grow. It is now the county seat of Douglas County, Kansas. The population of the town was estimated to be 82,120 in 2003.

Lawrence is known as the city where basketball began. Dr. James Naismith invented the game and brought it to the University of Kansas in 1898. It's also the home of the Haskell Indian Nations University, one of the best Native American colleges in the country. The University of Kansas is located there, too, and the poet Langston Hughes also lived in Lawrence.

Ashland, Oregon

A third pioneer town, Ashland, Oregon, began in yet a different way. Up until the winter of 1851–52, the Bear Creek Valley in the southernmost part of the Oregon Territory was inhabited only by small bands of Takelma Indians. The fertile valley was well protected by the Cascades on the east and the Sikiyou Mountains on the west. The

LAWRENCE MASSACRE

The conflict between pro- and antislavery forces grew worse after the Civil War started and Kansas voted to be a free state. Before dawn on August 21, 1863, 400 men from Missouri, led by William Quantrill, rode into Lawrence. Their purpose was "to burn every house and kill every man."

They didn't accomplish that, but in a few hours, they killed at least 150 men and older boys. Many were dragged from their homes and killed in front of their families. The raiders set most of the town's businesses on fire and looted the bank. Over 100 homes burned to the ground, and many more were partially burned.

We were afraid they would come out our way and burn the house. But they went the other way, so we were peaceful and safe. The next day, we went to see the awful sight. It was indeed awful to see our quiet little Lawrence in such a condition and the poor mortals that were taken and killed, all so suddenly, and no help to save. It was a time that will never be forgotten. I went into a church and it was full of the dead. Their faces were almost black, so dark one could not tell who they were. Women and girls crying, going about uncovering faces to see if any of their dear ones were among them.

—Mary Jane Cantrell, a resident of Lawrence at the time of the massacre, 1864

As soon as they had buried the dead, the brave people of the town set to work rebuilding. A number of buildings were finished that fall. By winter, Lawrence was beginning to look like a town again.

U.S. Army forces in Kansas and Western Missouri were under the command of General Thomas Ewing Jr. To get even with the raiders from Missouri, he ordered that three and a half Missouri counties bordering on Kansas be *depopulated*. This meant that thousands of people who lived in those counties were forced to leave their homes, which were then burned, along with planted fields. The whole area was devastated and became known as the "Burnt District."

Quantrill's raiders killing people on the streets of Lawrence, Kansas.

Library of Congress
LC-USZ62-134452

Indians moved around the valley, fishing, hunting game, and gathering edible plants.

Then gold was discovered at nearby Rich Gulch. News spread quickly, and a tent city grew up on the banks of Jackson Creek. Soon farmers from all over the country arrived to claim land under the Donation Land Claim Act of 1850. This was similar to the Homestead Act of 1862, but only included land in the Oregon Territory. Single men could claim 320 acres, but married ones got 640 acres. To get the property, they had to build a home and work the land.

Jackson County, where Ashland is located, was opened for settlement under this act. The first to arrive were Robert Hargadine and Sylvester Pease. They made a claim and built a log cabin at the end of Bear Creek Valley in what is now Ashland. Several others soon filed claims nearby.

A large group of settlers brought several thousand head of livestock with them in late 1853. There were 700 men, women, and children in the group.

Men pan for gold in a stream.
Library of Congress
LC-DIG-ppmsc-02669

Abel Helman and Eber Emery built a sawmill on the banks of Ashland Creek. They then could saw lumber to build houses. The next year, M. B. Morris joined them, building a flour mill in the same area. Houses grew up around the mills, and people called this area the Plaza. Nearby farmers came to buy lumber or to trade their wheat for flour.

The California-Oregon Trail passed through the area, so many pioneers visited the community on their way to California. Other stores and businesses grew up on the Plaza to serve these travelers as well as the townspeople. The owners of these businesses built homes nearby. The town grew slowly, and people who came usually stayed.

The town was first called Ashland Mills when the post office was built in 1855, but the word Mills was dropped in 1871. There were settlers from both Ashland, Ohio, and Ashland, Kentucky, so it's unclear which place it was named for.

In 1859, the town's population was just 50. Someone built a hotel to accommodate the travelers going to California. In 1869 a school was built, and then other businesses opened, including the Ashland Woolen Mills.

The Methodist Episcopal Church was organized in 1864. And after a conference there in 1869, they decided Ashland would be a fine place for a college. Ashland College and Normal School, for training teachers, was built.

During the 1870s and 1880s, Ashland grew faster than any other community south of Portland. Farming there was profitable, and agriculture became the main industry in the area. The town was incorporated in 1874 when there were 300 people. By 1880, there were 854 people.

The coming of the railroad in 1884 was important to the town. Now the people had a practical way to transport their crops and products to sell in other places. There were already a number of apple, pear, and peach orchards with thousands of trees. The railroad gave farmers a way to export their fruit.

A bank, two schools, a college, two hotels, a laundry, and a bakery had opened by the late 1880s. There were also five saloons, a doctor, and a dentist.

In 2007, the population was estimated at 21,630. Ashland is about 15 miles from the California border and not far from the Oregon coast. It's also close to Crater Lake National Park.

All across the country, towns like Walnut Grove, Lawrence, and Ashland grew up. Some grew to be big cities, and some remained small towns. They are all different, yet they're all alike in many ways.

COMMUNITY POSTER

You've read about three pioneer communities in different parts of the country. Now see what you can learn about your own community.

What You Need

Poster board
Markers or crayons

━◄●►━

Divide your poster board into two halves. Label one side THEN. Label the other side NOW.

Research the history of your town. Who was the first settler? When did he or she come? What kind of houses did people live in at first? What did they eat? What did they do for fun? What kind of work did they do?

To find the answers, you can ask older people or visit a local library or museum. If you have access to the Internet, you may find out some things online that you didn't know about your town.

Draw pictures to answer the questions, or if you can find pictures of early days in your community, you can use those.

On the NOW side, put pictures that answer the same questions for your community right now.

5

Pioneer Men

When a pioneer family finally reached the place they were going to call home, there were a lot of things for the father to think about. Housing was one. He usually built a temporary house to last until he could get some crops in if it wasn't too late in the year.

Most pioneer men, especially the homesteaders, were farmers. Whether the family was settling on the prairie or in a wooded area, clearing the land was difficult. In wooded areas like Ohio, Indiana, Wisconsin, or Minnesota, the land had to be cleared of trees. This was a very difficult, time-consuming job.

There were two ways to clear the land. One way was how the Native Americans did it: by *girdling* the trees. They cut a wide gash around the tree down low and peeled off the bark. The cut stopped the sap from flowing and, in time, killed the tree. The problem with this method was having to plant around the trees until they died. However, it didn't take long for the leaves to die so they didn't shade the soil, allowing crops to grow.

The other way pioneers cleared land was sometimes called the *New England method*: trees were cut down with an ax. This left stumps, which they either burned or dug out. After they felled the trees, they often used a two-man crosscut saw to cut the tree trunks into logs.

Besides the trees, there were lots of bushes and brush to be cleared. Much of the brush and wood was piled up and burned. Most men could only clear two or three acres a year. After the land was cleared, the soil had to be prepared for planting.

All the work had to be done with hand tools. It was hard work and took a long time.

Those who settled on the prairies didn't need to worry about clearing the land. Planting crops on the prairie had its own problems, though. The prairie sod was very hard to plow because the grasses had long and tangled roots. That made it hard to cut through it with a plow. Settlers heard popping noises the first time the sod was plowed. The sounds came from the deep roots snapping underground. Some people thought it sounded like the ripping of cloth.

Very early settlers on the prairie tried using the cast iron plows, pulled by oxen or horses, that they had brought from the East. These didn't work well because the soil stuck to the blades of the plow, causing the plow to get stuck in the mud. The farmer had to stop every few minutes to scrape off the blades.

In 1837, John Deere invented the self-scouring plow made of steel. (*Scouring* means scraping

(left) Pioneer men plowing on the prairie.
Library of Congress LC-USZ62-53987

(center) Pioneers used axes to chop down trees.
Photo by author

(right) Clearing trees using a crosscut saw.
Library of Congress LC-USZ62-61823

Copyright, 1886, by William Stanley. **A Breaking Scene of the Western Pioneers.**

SAWING INTO LOGS.

off.) The soil would fall off the blades as the plow cut through the sod. Farmers used a kind of self-scouring plow called a *moldboard plow*. It had a single sharp blade that cut through the sod, with a board behind. The board turned over a strip of earth as it went. This covered the sod and exposed the fertile topsoil.

After the fields were plowed, they were *harrowed*. The harrow was a heavy, V-shaped board that was dragged over the plowed field. It broke the soil down into finer pieces to make it easier to plant in.

Planting and Harvesting

Most planting was done by hand. Sometimes a farmer would carry a bag of seed over his shoulder and walk up and down the furrows, scattering seed. This was called *broadcasting*. Sometimes farmers used a *broadcast seeder*, which was a bag of seed with a star-shaped disc in the bottom. When the farmer turned a crank, seed fell out.

Wheat was one of the most important grain crops of the pioneers. Wheat was important for flour, to make bread. Other grains planted included barley, oats, and rye. The horses ate oats, and oats were made into oatmeal. Corn was another important crop. It provided food and feed for animals. It was planted later in the spring than the other grains, and it didn't need as much care as other grain crops.

Most livestock roamed free, so farmers had to protect their fields from the animals. If there was wood nearby, trees were cut down. The logs were split into rails to build fences.

A man and boy plow on the prairie with two horses.
Library of Congress LC-USZ62-127591

An old-fashioned harrow that farmers used to break up soil after plowing.
Photo by author, courtesy of Garst Museum, Greenville, Ohio

(left) **Men with scythes cut the prairie grass.**
Library of Congress LC-USZ62-100538

(center) **Rail fences that looked like this were built to keep livestock out of the fields.**
Photo by author

(right) **Men throw hay on a hay wagon after cutting it.**
Library of Congress LC-USZ62-58354

I have sowd seventeen bushels of wheat and seven bushels of oats and are a going to plant about ten acres with corn. . . . I have got about one acre to plant with potatoes that is plowed. I have not planted much garden yet.

—Ephraim Fairchild, in a letter he wrote home from Iowa, May 1857

By June, the farmers began cutting prairie grass to dry for cattle feed and livestock bedding. They cut the tall grass with a *scythe*, which was a tool with a long wooden handle and a long blade. It took two hands to use the scythe, which the farmer would swing back and forth to cut the grass. A *sickle* was a similar tool, but it was much smaller and its blade was curved so that it could be used with one hand.

When the small grains were ready to harvest, farmers used a cradle, a thin post with four parallel fingers, which they attached to the handle of the scythe. Each time they swung the scythe, the cradle held the cut grain, allowing them to lay it in neat rows. Then it was easy to rake the stalks into piles. Next, the stalks were bundled together with bands of straw, called *shocks*. These shocks were then dried.

When the grain was dry, it had to be *threshed*, or separated from the stalk. There were a couple of ways to thresh. Some people drove a team of oxen or horses over and around the stalks until the grain fell out. They had to turn the bundles often to get as much grain out as possible, a process called *treading*.

The other way to thresh was hitting the stalks with a *flail*. A flail was a long wooden pole. Attached to the pole with a short piece of leather was a shorter wooden pole. The farmer swung the long pole around, causing the small pole to hit the piles of grain, which loosened the husks. It worked best on a hard-packed dirt floor. Board floors had spaces between the boards, and some of the grain would be lost. Farmers had to turn the grain often with a hayfork to make sure they got all the grain out.

When they finished, farmers gathered up the straw to be used as bedding for the animals. What was left on the floor was the grain and the *chaff*, which was the hulls and beards of the grain. These needed to be separated from the grain by *winnowing*. The mixture was tossed into the air with scoops or baskets. The wind blew away the chaff, and the heavier grain fell back into the container. Sometimes farmers used a screen to separate the grain from the chaff.

Farmers used a corn knife to pick corn. They laid the ears of corns, with their husks on, in the barn to dry. Later they would have a husking bee, where neighbors came and helped remove the husks with a tool called a *husking pin*. This was a time for fun and fellowship as well as work.

Grain couldn't be used for food until it was ground. It was a very hard job to grind it by hand. Wheat could be ground using a *mortar and pestle*. The mortar was a hollowed-out stump and the pestle was a smooth piece of wood attached to a lever. It was used to pound the grain until it was fine. But it took hours to grind enough to make a loaf of bread.

Soon there were mills in most areas, which made grinding grain much easier. The mill could be 50 to 100 miles away, so a farmer would load his grain onto a wagon, and a horse pulled it to the mill. Sometimes he went on horseback, with bags of grain across the horse's back in front of him. He was often gone several days.

> I have been a thrashing this week. Harvesting we had [115] bushels wheat. They use thrashing machines here. It requires 8 horses and ten men to tend them and will thrash from 3 to 5 hundred [bushels] a day . . . it's a right smart machine.
>
> —*John Kenyon, in a letter home, 1856*

Trouble for Farmers

Unfortunately, the plowing, planting, and harvesting did not always go smoothly. Many things could go wrong. Like today's farmers, pioneer farmers were at the mercy of the weather.

Drought was a big cause of crop failure. When there wasn't enough rain, the soil dried out, and

Pioneers sometimes had to beat out a prairie fire to keep it from destroying their homes.
Library of Congress LC-USZ62-62759

(left) **Wolves were often seen by the pioneers.**
Photo by author

(right) **This pioneer family's livestock was important enough that they wanted their animals included in the family photograph.**
Library of Congress
LC-DIG-ppmsca-08371

crops didn't grow well. Sometimes cattle died because there wasn't enough hay to feed them. Also, droughts in the prairie often caused dust storms, and sometimes fires raged across the prairie when it was dry.

During the 1870s, many areas were plagued by grasshoppers (see page 61). They ate many of the crops, so farmers didn't have enough food for their families. They also didn't have any extra crops to sell.

Pioneers also had to worry about physical harm. Wild animals like wolves and snakes were always a danger.

In some places, Indian raids were a problem. They didn't happen nearly as often as many people think, but there was always a threat. Occasionally Indians would raid an area, burn the crops and homes, and kill some of the people. In some cases, the settlers initiated attacks on the Indians.

Livestock and Wild Game

Besides planting and harvesting crops, a farmer also had livestock to care for. Many families had a cow to provide milk to drink and to make butter and cheese. Hogs were fairly easy to raise. In spring, summer, and fall they were often turned loose to graze in the woods. Chickens were common on the frontier, too. They provided eggs for the family and extra ones to sell. And when a hen stopped laying, she provided a good meal for the family.

Hunting was also the job of pioneer men. In the early years, game was plentiful, and hunters had no trouble supplying the family with meat. On the plains, it was possible to hunt buffalo, which would provide food for a family for a long time. *Venison*—deer meat—was a common food for pioneers because of the number of deer. Pioneers also hunted rabbits and squirrels for food.

Pioneer men had different types of work to do according to the season. In the spring, before it was time to plow and plant, many farmers tapped their maple trees. Then they boiled down the sap to make syrup and sugar.

During the summer, pioneer men would be busy weeding the crops, tending the garden, and repairing and improving the house and other buildings. Late summer and early fall found them harvesting the crops, chopping wood, and doing other tasks to get ready for winter.

During the winter, farmers had a bit more time for other tasks. They still had to tend to their livestock every day and split wood for the stove or fireplace. It took a lot of wood to heat the house and cook the food for a family. Farmers also spent time in winter repairing tools, harnesses, and other items.

TRACKING ANIMALS

We don't see as many wild animals as the pioneers did, but we can often see where animals have been. All you have to do is look for their tracks. In most areas, you won't find bear tracks or wolf tracks. In many places, though, you might see tracks of deer, raccoons, opossums, squirrels, muskrat, mink, and beavers. Study the tracks below, then go out and see how many tracks you can find. Record your observations in your journal (see page 35).

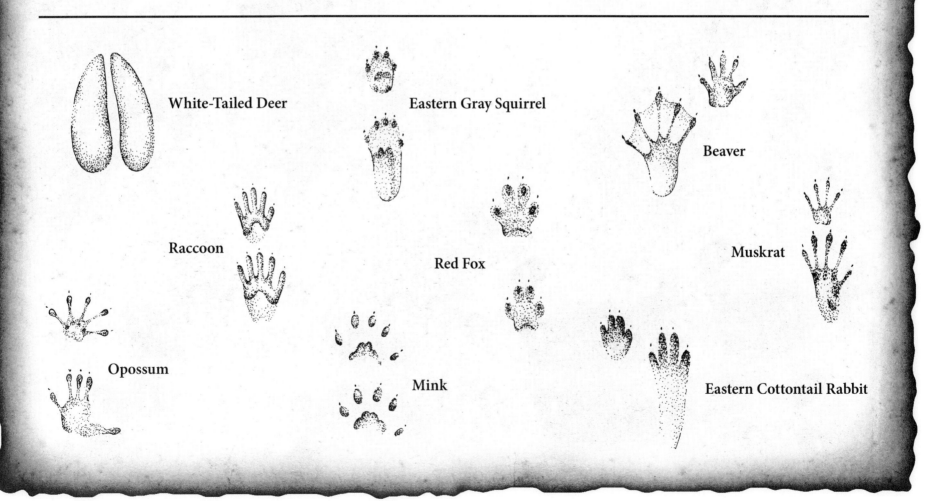

White-Tailed Deer

Eastern Gray Squirrel

Beaver

Raccoon

Red Fox

Muskrat

Opossum

Mink

Eastern Cottontail Rabbit

MAKE MAPLE SNOW CANDY

If you've ever read Laura Ingalls Wilder's *Little House in the Big Woods*, you know about making maple snow candy. You can do it, too, with a little help from an adult. And you don't have to wait till winter—you can use shaved ice or vanilla ice cream instead of snow!

What You Need

Cookie sheet
Pure maple syrup (other pancake syrup
  will not work)
Saucepan
Big spoon
Snow, shaved ice, or ice cream

Put a cookie sheet in the freezer to get cold.

Pour some maple syrup into a saucepan. A cup of syrup will make plenty of candy for several people. Heat on a stove until the syrup begins to boil. Let it boil 3 or 4 minutes for soft, chewy candy, or 6 minutes for hard, brittle candy. It should be stirred every couple of minutes. Have an adult do this.

Spread fresh, packed snow, shaved ice, or ice cream on the cold cookie sheet. Carefully dribble a thin stream of hot syrup in lines over the snow. You might want to write your name or make a picture.

The candy will harden immediately. Once cooled, pick up a piece and try it.

GEORGE WASHINGTON BUSH
AFRICAN AMERICAN SETTLER, c.1790-1863

George Washington Bush was born in Philadelphia sometime around 1790. Like many slaves, he wasn't sure when he was born. His father was an African American sailor and his mother was an Irish house maid. His father inherited money from the man he had worked for as a servant for years. Not much more is known about Bush's early life.

Bush served under Andrew Jackson in the Battle of New Orleans in 1815. Then he became a fur trapper and mountain man in the Oregon Territory. He worked for the Hudson's Bay Company until 1829.

In 1830 he settled in Missouri after inheriting a good bit of money from his parents. He married Isabella James, a German woman whose father was a Baptist minister. He did well on his farm, and they had 10 sons in the next 12 years. Only five survived.

At the time, Missouri was a slave state, and most white people didn't treat black people well, even if they were free. So the Bushes decided to move to Oregon, and joined four white families for the trip west. They left in May 1844. Bush acted as the guide for the group. He took five wagons, and he also helped finance some of the other people who went. The trip went well, and the group reached the Columbia River that fall. Then they learned that the Oregon Territory had a law against black settlers.

Bush's friends would not settle where he and his family were not welcome, so they all crossed the Columbia River and settled on the north bank. The land there belonged to the British Hudson's Bay Company, and the British agent apparently allowed the settlement. Some said it was because the agent had a Native American wife and was familiar with prejudice.

The next year, the whole group took up a claim for land south of Puget Sound. That land is now part of the state of Washington. First called New Market, the town was later named Tumwater. It was the first permanent American settlement in the state of Washington.

Bush died at the age of 84. He was remembered as a kind and generous man who inspired all who knew him.

[George Washington Bush] was a true American and yet without a country; he owed allegiance to the flag and yet the flag would not own him; he was firmly held to obey the law and yet the law would not protect him, and his oath would not be taken in a court of law.

—*Ezra Meeker,*
Washington State historian

(top) **An old mill that is still being used to grind grain into flour and meal.**

Photo by author

(bottom) **A millstone ground the grain into flour or meal.**

Photo by author, courtesy Garst Museum, Greenville, Ohio

Tradesmen

Although the majority of the men who moved west lived off the land, many others followed a trade or profession. Every small town had a number of tradesmen, as well as merchants and other workers.

The blacksmith was very important in a pioneer town. He could do almost anything with iron. One of his most important tasks was making horseshoes and shoeing horses and oxen. Almost every farmer owned these animals and used them in his farming. It was important for their feet to be protected with shoes.

The first homes were created without nails, but they were soon in demand. So blacksmiths made nails, along with latches, hinges, carpenter's tools, and hoops for the barrels the cooper made. They also made cooking utensils and fireplace tools.

A blacksmith had a raised brick hearth known as a *forge*. In it he built a fire with charcoal to heat the iron. Huge bellows fanned the fire and kept it burning brightly. The smith used several different-sized hammers to pound the hot iron on an anvil to shape it into tools. He also poured *molten*, or melted, iron into molds to make some objects.

A tinsmith was another important metal worker in a pioneer town. He started with a sheet of tin, which is a soft, silvery-white metal, and used a hammer to shape the sheets into cups, pitchers, tableware, and other objects. One of his most important products was the lantern. It was often made with fancy patterns of stars or flowers on the sides. These were made by punching holes through the tin with a nail. The holes let light through but were small enough so that the wind couldn't blow out the light when the farmer took it to the barn or outhouse.

The gristmill was important to the early settlers, so every town had a miller. It was a hard, time-consuming job to grind grain into flour by hand. The pioneers had to use a mortar and pestle, and it might take hours to grind enough grain to make one loaf of bread. But once there was a mill, farmers took their grain there to be ground into flour or meal. Farmers began growing more grain and selling the extra flour.

The mill was usually located on the edge of a river or stream. A dam was built across the water to make a millpond. The water flowed into buckets on a huge waterwheel, which caused it to turn. A set of gears carried the energy from the turning wheel to the millstone, and as the millstone was turned by the gears it would grind the grain.

The sawmill was usually one of the first businesses in a new settlement. Most settlers' first homes were log cabins, but they wanted to move up to frame houses eventually. And for that, they needed wooden planks rather than round logs.

It was possible for two men with a whipsaw to cut a log into a plank. A platform had to be built, then one man stood on the platform above the log. The other man stood below, and they pushed and pulled the saw back and forth until they had flattened one side of the log. This took quite a while, and the whole process had to be repeated on all four sides of the log. Thousands of planks were needed by the settlers in one community.

Not only were plank houses easier to build than log cabins, they were better to live in. The settlers didn't have to worry about wind and snow blowing in between the logs. It was easy to build wooden floors in a plank or frame house. Two-story houses could also be built.

A sawmill worked about the same as the gristmill. Water from the millpond turned a wheel, which then turned a saw, which cut the wood. After a while, all the trees near the sawmill had been felled, so the owner paid farmers in the area to cut trees in the woods during the winter. When spring came, they put the logs in the river, and the logs floated down to the mill.

The General Store and More

A pioneer town's general store often used the *barter system*, which was a system of trading goods without money. Farmers brought their produce and other items to the store. The storekeeper put a price on all the goods, kept records of what people brought in, and what they traded them for.

The store was also a meeting place for the community. People would sit around the potbelly stove and discuss the news. In summer, they sat on the porch. The post office was often located in a corner of the store.

The *cooper* was a busy man, too. He made wooden barrels, tubs, and buckets. The cooper was important because the pioneers kept almost everything in barrels. Even liquids were stored in watertight barrels.

The cooper bought barrel planks from the sawmill, then planed each plank into the perfect shape so they would fit together tightly. The tops and bottoms of the planks were narrower and the middle was the widest part. With all the pieces

standing upright, a wooden hoop was used to hold them together temporarily. The cooper then put permanent metal hoops around the top, middle, and bottom of the barrel. He usually got those hoops from the blacksmith. He then made circles of wood for the top and bottom. If dry goods were to be stored in the barrel, he made a removable top. If it was to hold liquid, he sealed the barrel and cut a hole in the top so the liquid could be poured in. Then he cut another hole down low on one side and put in a *spigot*, which is like a faucet. When someone turned the spigot, the liquid would come out.

Tubs and buckets were made in much the same way. The main difference was that the planks were made narrower at the bottom and left wide in the middle and at the top. They were also held together with hoops. Tubs and buckets didn't need a top.

The shoemaker in those days was called a *cobbler*. He made new shoes and repaired old ones.

The shoes worn by settlers were all made by hand. A cobbler measured the person's feet, then got to work. He cut the leather, then hand-sewed the top. Sometimes the soles were sewn to the

(left) **Sawmills created lumber needed to build houses.**
Library of Congress LC-DIG-ppmsca-17296

(above) **Barrels were sometimes used to catch rainwater that ran off the roof.**
Photo by author

A cobbler works on shoes as a child watches.
Library of Congress LC-USZ62-74307

uppers, but more often they were nailed on with wooden pegs.

People worked hard in those days, and they spent a lot of time walking and standing, so their shoes wore out quickly. The cobbler had lots of work. He often made other leather items, such as belts.

The *wheelwright*'s job was to make wheels, particularly wagon wheels. He started by making a round piece of wood to use for the *hub*, or center of the wheel. Wood from the elm tree was often used because the cross-grain made it strong enough that it wouldn't split under strain.

Next, the wheelwright drilled holes all the way around the rim of the hub for the spokes. Most wagon wheels had 14 spokes, which were carved from ash or oak. They fit very tightly when he tapped them into the holes. The other end of the

spokes fit tightly into holes in wooden arches called *fellies*. The fellies joined together to make a perfect circle.

When the wooden part of the wheel was finished, it was time for the blacksmith's help. The wheel was set up over a pit of water. A red-hot strip of iron called a *strake* was laid on top of the wheel rim. It had holes punched for nails, and while the iron was still hot, the wheelwright pounded in big nails. Then he turned the wheel so the part with the strake was in the cold water. That caused the iron to cool and tighten on the wheel. While that was happening, he was putting on another strake—there were usually six altogether. The iron rims made the wheels last longer. The wheelwright made other kinds of wheels, as well, and also repaired all types of broken wheels.

Carpenters in pioneer times were known as *joiners*. A joiner often worked with the owner to finish the inside of a new frame house. He built cupboards and cabinets and furniture. He often built the staircase in a two-story house, and if there was no sawmill, he also planed down planks to the right size.

When the village began to grow, a printer often moved in and started a newspaper. All the type had to be set by hand. (Some printers had a young man, called a *printer's devil*, as an apprentice. He was there to learn the trade.) Each letter was made separately from metal, and they had to be placed backward so they would print right. The printer had to put each letter in the *galley*, which was a long tray to hold type that had already been set. He put shorter pieces of metal between words so there would be spaces. A skilled printer could set about 1,000 characters in an hour. Characters included letters, numbers, punctuation marks, and the spaces between letters.

The galley was held together with an iron frame to hold the type in place. Then it was placed in the press, and the printer spread ink over it. A piece of paper was placed on top of the inked galley, and when it was pressed down, the letters were transferred to the paper.

In 1883, the *linotype machine* was invented. After that, printers didn't have to set type one letter at a time. Setting type with a linotype machine was five times faster than setting it by hand.

Inns, Churches, and Schools

Roads in the 1800s were made of dirt or sometimes logs (log roads were called *corduroy roads*), and this made travel very slow. Travelers needed places to spend the night along their journeys. When a village had grown and had other types of businesses, an inn was sometimes built for those passing through to stay in. Besides a bed, an inn provided meals for weary travelers. People in the village also enjoyed going to the inn for entertainment or drinks.

The dining room usually had tables and benches. The more expensive bedrooms provided sheets on the beds. A cheaper room might just have a straw mattress on the floor without sheets. You didn't always have a room by yourself, either—often three or more strangers slept in the same room.

When churches were set up in the village, they needed preachers. Often congregations could not afford to pay a full-time preacher, so they used a circuit rider (see page 58). Sometimes a church

An old-time print shop.
Photo by author, courtesy Garst Museum, Greenville, Ohio

back east would send a preacher west to start a new church in a pioneer community. Often these men would have wives and children, which brought new families into the community.

Schoolteachers in pioneer days were most often men. They needed to be strong enough to discipline the big boys who attended school in the winter. The teacher at first was paid by the parents, but also boarded with different families.

There were other occupations, too, but these were the most common on the frontier. As you can see, no matter what a pioneer man did for a living, his job was never easy.

6
Pioneer Women

It took a special kind of woman to succeed on the frontier. Taking care of a family in pioneer days was a difficult job. Most pioneer families were large, and most of the work had to be done by hand.

Some women were excited about the move west. One of these was Miriam Thompson Tuller, who married Arthur Thompson when she was 18. She said her husband was "fired with patriotism," and "I was possessed with a spirit of adventure and a desire to see what was new and strange." However, her story did not have a happy ending.

In the fall of 1848, when gold was discovered in California my husband went as did many others, to seek gold, but never returned. He was murdered by the Indians.

—*Miriam Thompson Tuller,*
in the last entry in her diary, 1848

Some women were dead set against the trip and very unhappy that their husbands expected them to go west. But in the 1800s, men were definitely the heads of the households. The women often had no say in these kinds of decisions.

> Dr. Wilson [her husband] has determined to go to California. I am going with him, as there is no other alterative. . . . Oh, my dear Mother. . . . I thought that I felt bad when I wrote you . . . from Independence, but it was nothing like this.
>
> —*Margaret Hereford Wilson,*
> *in a letter to her mother, 1850*

For many women, moving to the frontier was like stepping back in time. Most had fairly comfortable homes in the East. They had glass windows, rugs, nice furniture, and curtains on their windows. It was a big change to go from living in a house like that to living in a dugout or soddy on the prairie, or a log cabin in the woods.

Life and Death on the Trail

Before 1840, there were not many non–Native American women west of the Mississippi. A few had traveled the Santa Fe Trail to New Mexico with their husbands. Another handful of women had gone west with their fur-trader husbands. But it wasn't until people heard of free land in the Northwest that women began moving west in large numbers. Narcissa Whitman and Eliza Spalding had been the first white women to cross the Rocky Mountains (see page 34). As missionaries traveling with their husbands, they paved the way for other women to go west.

The months on the trail were grueling for everyone. The women still had to do most of the tasks they did at home, though they were more difficult on the trail. Instead of a cookstove, the women had to make a campfire to cook on. But first, she had to gather wood or buffalo chips to burn.

(left) **A woman kneels by the campfire to cook.**
Library of Congress
LC-USZ62-101763

(right) **A California gold mine.**
Library of Congress
LC-DIG-ppmsc-04825

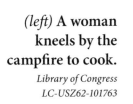

By the time one has squatted around the fire, and cooked bread and bacon, and made several dozen trips to and from the wagon—washed the dishes (with no place to drain them) and gotten things ready for an early breakfast, some of the others already have their nightcaps on.

—*Helen Carpenter,*
about cooking on the trail, 1857

Clothing on the trail was a problem for women. At the time, hoop skirts were the style. Helen Carpenter said she certainly "would not recommend [hoops] for this mode of traveling." Most women abandoned their hoops after a short time on the trail. Then their dresses dragged on the ground and got dusty or muddy, often catching on briars and other plants. Long skirts could get caught in wagon wheels or catch fire from the campfire. A few women began wearing bloomers to avoid these problems. Most women thought bloomers were immodest and that they would cause the men to talk if they wore them.

Pioneer women had to do laundry whenever they had the chance. Wagon trains would stop every two weeks or so for the women to spend a day washing clothes. This was not an easy job, as they had to beat the clothes on rocks in a stream or fill tubs with water and heat them to boiling over a campfire.

⬥ FEMALE HOMESTEADERS ⬥

Although most homesteaders were men, a few single women filed claims. That number included the Chrisman sisters of Nebraska. The sisters—Hattie, Lizzie, Lutie, and Ruth—had moved west with their parents and brothers in 1883. Lizzie filed a claim for a homestead in 1887. Her sister, Lutie, filed her claim the next year. Their father built them sod houses, and they took turns living with each other. That way they could fulfill the residence requirements without having to live alone. Hattie and Ruth were younger, so they had to wait to file.

Some female teachers held down homestead claims while they were teaching. Teacher Pauline Shoemaker came from Pennsylvania to North Dakota in 1902. After teaching several years, she filed a claim. She said, "I have done everything else. I might as well try homesteading." Her homestead was located along the Knife River. Three years later she married a neighbor.

In 1907, 11.9 percent of homesteaders were women. Of these women, it is reported that 42.4 percent of them fulfilled the requirements to claim their land. In contrast, only 37 percent of the men who filed claims eventually received title to the land.

A schoolmistress greets her students outside the school.

Library of Congress
LC-USZ62-104627

Women wait on shore while the wagons cross the Platte River.

Library of Congress LC-USZ62-49128

made a deafening terrible noise. As is their habit in stampeding, they did not turn out of their course for anything. Some of our wagons were within their line of advance and in consequence one was completely demolished and two were overturned.

—Catherine Haun, 1849

Accidents on the trail were fairly common. People were injured by the livestock, run over by the wagons, and hurt in falls.

Camilla and I both burnt our arms very badly while washing. They were red and swollen and painful as though scalded with boiling water. I do not see that there is any way of preventing it, for everything has to be done in the wind and the sun.

—Rebecca Ketcham, 1853

And of course, a mother had to take care of her children. Most felt their main job on the trip west was keeping the family together, and tried to provide some sort of normal family life for their children. One of the worst things that could happen to a mother on the trail was to lose a child or a husband. People died from accidents, buffalo stampedes, and Indian attacks.

One day a herd [of buffalo] came in our direction like a great black cloud . . . advancing toward us very swiftly and with wild snorts, noses almost to the ground and tails flying in midair. . . . [They]

On the afternoon of this day . . . the hem of my dress caught on an axle-handle, precipitating me under the wheels both of which passed over me, badly crushing the left leg, before Father could stop the oxen.

—Catherine Sager, age 12 in 1844

Crossing raging rivers with the wagons and livestock was a constant danger. Many people and animals drowned while fording the rivers.

The last branch we rode as much as half a mile in crossing and against the current too, which made it hard for the horses, the water being up to their sides. Husband had considerable difficulty in crossing the cart. Both cart and mules were turned upside down in the river and entangled in the harness. The mules would have drowned but for a desperate struggle to get them ashore.

—Narcissa Whitman, 1836

Indian attacks did occur, but did not cause nearly as many deaths as disease and accidents. Pamelia Fergus, who traveled west to meet her husband, wrote that she slept with a gun at her side. She was afraid because of the reports that Sioux and Crow were attacking wagon trains. But the biggest danger of Indian attack came when a person or small group was separated from the wagon train. Natives almost never attacked a wagon train in a circle formation.

In one case, a family was separated from the wagon train when they stopped to bury the father of the family, who had died of cholera. While they were digging the grave, Indians attacked them and killed or captured all but the mother and a five-year-old daughter. They wandered for three days before they came upon another wagon train.

Without a doubt, disease was the biggest killer on the westward journey. (See page 30 for more information about diseases on the trail.) Head and body lice were also a problem. The pioneers seldom had a chance to bathe, and lice thrive on dirty bodies. These insects cause constant itching.

Nature handed its share of problems to the pioneers, too. Besides the rivers and mountains they had to cross, weather could be a problem. Rain made cooking over a campfire difficult. One woman said that on rainy days, there was "nothing to eat but crackers and raw bacon." But others held umbrellas over the fires. Some built the fire under a large hanging pot so the pot would shelter the fire from the rain.

Settlers dreaded thunderstorms. Amelia Stewart Knight reported that "a dreadful storm of rain and hail . . . and very sharp lightning" killed

two oxen. "The winde was so high," she said, "I thought it would tear the wagon to pieces."

> **Deliver me from a thunder storm of the plaines. . . . I will assure you we had eight cotton stuffed comforters wet through and not a dry rag to put on . . .** everything was wet in the wagon through a thick blanket and cover.
>
> —*Pamelia Fergus, 1864*

Settling Down

When the pioneer woman finally settled in her new home at the end of the trail, things improved. However, living conditions were rarely as good as those at home had been.

Whether she lived in a dugout, a soddy, or a log cabin or house, the pioneer woman had a lot of work to do. And no matter what kind of house she had, she tried to make it into a comfortable home. She sometimes *whitewashed* the walls by painting them with a mixture of lime, chalk, and water. Sometimes she papered them with newspapers or covered them with fabric.

Bertha Anderson, who settled in Montana, whitewashed her home's walls. When the family had a little more money, she bought calico cloth and tacked it on the wall. She even hung a cheesecloth curtain with crocheted lace. She didn't like her little ones playing on the rough plank floor, so she made rugs. She used every available scrap of material, even going to the dump to find flour sacks. She dyed them brown, cut them in strips, and sewed the strips together. A woman named Mrs. Kemmis, who had a loom, wove them into

A pioneer loom.
Photo by author, courtesy Garst Museum, Greenville, Ohio

A woman prepares to cook a meal in the fireplace.

Photo by author, courtesy Darke County Parks, Greenville Ohio

rugs. Bertha didn't have much furniture, but she wrote in later years, "We liked our home, maybe better than some rich people liked theirs."

Some people brought a good bit of furniture with them in their wagons, and the wealthy shipped their furniture to the new homes. Some had left home with cook stoves, iron beds, and pianos, all of which they had to abandon along the trail to lighten the load for the oxen.

So pioneers made their own furniture when they arrived at their new homes. Stools were made from a log split in half. The top was smoothed off, and then wooden pegs served as legs. Bed frames were made from wood, with slats across. Mattresses filled with hay, feathers, or cornhusks were used. Trunks sometimes were used as tables. Often boards would be placed across two trunks, making a large table where the whole family could eat.

The earliest pioneer houses were lit by candles and the fire in the fireplace. Some families used a grease lamp. This was a metal dish filled with animal fat, sometimes bear or hog grease. They twisted a piece of cloth and put one end in the grease, then lit the other end. However, grease lamps didn't give much light, and they produced a lot of smoke.

From the 1860s on, oil or kerosene lamps were popular. The fuel was in the bottom of the lamp. The bottom of the wick was in the kerosene. They lit the other end of the wick. They controlled the height of the flame by turning a lever and making the wick longer or shorter. A glass globe usually covered the lamp.

Hard Work

A pioneer woman's work was never done. One of her biggest jobs was making sure her family was well fed. Her husband usually provided the meat for the family by hunting, fishing, and raising and butchering livestock. She and the children usually took care of the garden. Fresh vegetables were plentiful. All through the summer and into the fall, the family ate the vegetables straight from the garden. Pioneer women canned much of the garden produce to use in winter. Some goods, like onions, were hung to dry from the rafters. Potatoes, carrots, turnips, and other root vegetables were stored in the root cellar. Fresh milk, cream, butter, and cheese were kept in the springhouse or in the creek.

Churning butter was a weekly job. Often the children took turns pounding the dasher up and down in the churn. Some of the milk was made into cheese.

Most women started out cooking over a fire in the fireplace. Hooks were usually attached to the fireplace to hold pots. The hooks would swing back and forth, so she could move the pot over the fire, then back out of the fireplace. Much of the food was cooked in a Dutch oven, which was placed in the coals. Coals were piled on top of the lid so that the food could cook from the top and bottom. Cornbread, stew, and fruit cobbler were all cooked in Dutch ovens. Some food was cooked in a skillet.

CHURN YOUR OWN BUTTER

Pioneers churned their butter in a big wooden butter churn with a paddle called a dasher.
But you don't have to have a churn in order to make your own butter. Just follow this recipe.

What You Need

1 pint of heavy cream (let it set at room
temperature for 8 hours first)
1-quart jar with a lid that screws on tight
Bowl
Wooden spoon or spatula

Pour the cream into the jar. It should
be half full. Be sure the lid is
on tight, then shake the jar.
Don't shake too hard or too
fast—about one shake per
second is good. It will take a
while, so you might want
to have someone take
turns with you.

The cream will
get thick and coat

the jar. Keep on shaking. The cream will
eventually come off the sides of the jar
and start forming lumps of butter. When
you look into the jar and see a ball of
yellow butter in some liquid—that's the
buttermilk—it's ready.

Pour the butter and buttermilk into a
bowl. Use a wooden spoon or spatula to
press the ball of butter against the side
of the bowl to squeeze out all the buttermilk. Pour the buttermilk
into a jar and refrigerate. You
can drink it, or your
parents might want
to use it to make bis-
cuits or pancakes.

Rinse the butter with cold water. Again,
use the spoon to squeeze out all the water.
Put the butter on a small plate and put it
in the refrigerator if you're not ready to
eat it yet.

(*above*) **A woman spins wool into yarn.**

Courtesy Magritte Beale, Darke County Parks, Ohio

(*right*) **Hand-dipped candles.**

Photo by author

girls' clothing. Men's and boys' clothing was made from cotton, linen, or wool.

Women wore dresses with several petticoats under them. An apron was also part of every woman's outfit. It protected the dress from stains. A woman or girl could also use her apron to carry eggs, vegetables, or wood. Women wore long stockings and lace-up shoes. Women and girls wore sunbonnets outside to keep from getting sunburned, and they often wore other types of bonnets for special occasions.

Men and boys wore long pants with suspenders and long-sleeved shirts to work. Straw hats protected them from the sun. For special occasions they wore trousers with a shirt and a vest or a jacket. A felt hat replaced the straw hat.

When they first settled in the West, most people only had a couple of outfits. They had one outfit they wore every day while they were working. Then they had another, better outfit for church and other special occasions. They often went barefoot in warm weather to save their shoes.

In later years on the frontier, the general store stocked several kinds of fabric. Women could buy flannel, gingham, calico, denim, wool, linen, and muslin. The store also sold dye, scissors, needles, pins, and buttons.

Clothing was never thrown away. When children outgrew a garment, it was handed down to younger brothers and sisters. When a piece of clothing became too worn to wear any more, it was used for other things. Sometimes it was cut into strips and made into rag rugs. Other times it was used to make patchwork quilts.

Another job of the pioneer woman was making candles. They were sometimes made from

Pioneer women also had full charge of the family's clothes. Clothing had to be functional and wear well. It also had to be made from readily available materials. The mother had to make the clothing, launder it, and mend it. But before she could make clothing, she had to have cloth.

In early years on the frontier, many people spun wool into yarn or flax into linen thread using a spinning wheel. After this was done, the yarn or flax had to be woven into cloth. A common material was *linsey-woolsey*, which was a combination of linen and wool. The linen threads ran lengthwise and gave the cloth strength. The wool threads, which ran crosswise, made it warm. This fabric was popular because it wore well and was cheap, but it was a rather rough fabric and not very attractive.

Later on, the women bought cloth with which to make the family's clothing. Calico, a printed cotton material, was popular for women's and beeswax. More often they were made from *tallow*, or animal fat. The tallow had to be melted in a kettle, and then boiled in water. Next it was strained to get out any impurities. This made a better-smelling candle.

Wicks were made from cotton string. They were soaked in tallow and hung up to dry, so they would be stiff and straight. Then the wicks were usually tied to a piece of wood so they could be dipped into the tallow over and over. Often there were a number of wicks tied to one stick. They had to be dipped for a short time so they would be coated with a new coat of tallow. If left in the hot tallow too long, the tallow that was already on the wicks would melt.

Some people had candle molds in which to make their candles. Candles made in a mold were more uniform in shape. Cords were placed in the metal molds for wicks. Then the melted tallow was poured in. After it cooled and hardened, the candle was removed from the mold, and the wick was trimmed. This was an easier and faster way to make candles.

Candles were placed in candlestick holders or in lanterns. Some were placed in *sconces*, which were candle holders that hung on the wall.

Making soap was another job of a pioneer woman. She used lye and animal fat to make it. Lye was made from ashes. The ashes were placed in a barrel, called a *leach*, which had a small slit near the bottom. The barrel was tipped and water was poured in the top. A bucket was placed under the slit. The water that dripped out of the slit was lye. It was very dangerous, because it would burn your skin. It could also burn your throat if you breathed the fumes.

First, the tallow and water were boiled in a kettle, usually outside because of the fumes. Lye was added after the tallow melted. (Tallow kept the lye in the soap from burning the pioneers' skin.) Sometimes wild ginger or bayberry was added to make the soap smell nice. The heated, liquid soap was poured into a pan and left to cool and harden. The next day, it was cut it into bars.

Keeping the house neat and clean was quite a challenge in the early pioneer homes. Women did as well as they could. They swept the floors, whether dirt or wood, with brooms made from twigs or corn husks.

(left) **A little girl uses a candle to find her way to bed.**
Library of Congress LC-USZ62-77015

(below) **Pioneer women swept the hearth and the floors of the cabin with a hand-made broom.**
Photo by author, courtesy Darke County Parks, Greenville, Ohio

DIP CANDLES

It's fun to dip candles the way the pioneers did.
Instead of tallow, you'll use paraffin or old candles. You need help from an adult to melt the wax.

What You Need

Paraffin, or several old candles
Scissors
Double boiler, or large saucepan plus coffee can
Heavy string
Stick or pencil
Bucket of cold water

Cut the wax or candles into small pieces so they will melt faster.

Place wax in the top of a double boiler and put water in the bottom. If you don't have a double boiler, put the wax in the coffee can and set it in a pan of water. But never put wax in a pan directly over the burner. It could catch on fire.

Boil the water until the wax in the can is completely melted. Remove from stove. Be sure the wax is at least as deep as you want your candle to be long.

Cut the string into pieces about 15 inches long. Tie one end of the string around the stick. Then, dip the string into the wax. Leave it for just five seconds, then pull it out. Let it cool so it will stiffen. If the string floats, use another stick to poke it down into the wax.

Keep dipping the string into the wax. Only leave it in about three seconds each time. If you leave it in too long, the wax that is already on it will melt off. In between dipping in the wax, dip your candle in cold water. That helps it to cool faster.

You'll probably need to dip your candle about 25 times. When the candle is as thick as you want it, take it out of the wax. If it is lumpy, roll it on a table or other hard surface while it's still warm. Cut the bottom off so it will be flat and will stand in a candlestick, and cut the wick so it stands up about half an inch above the candle.

Your candle is now ready to light and enjoy!

Pioneer Social Life

Pioneer women did occasionally have a little time to enjoy themselves. Most women enjoyed just talking with other women more than anything else. Most didn't have any close neighbors and really missed the contact with other women that they had been used to back east.

Reading was another popular pastime for women on the frontier. The Bible was a favorite reading material. Magazines helped women to maintain contact with the world they had left. They also kept in touch with friends and relatives back home by writing letters—it was an exciting time when a letter from home arrived.

The church was important to pioneer women. Sunday services gave them a chance to get together with others, and they looked forward to church socials and picnics.

Groups of settlers organized other kinds of get-togethers, too. Dances were sometimes held in a hall or even in a church or school building. Square dancing was popular, complete with a fiddler. People would gather to dance, talk, eat, and have fun.

Quilting bees, also called *quiltings*, were enjoyed by many pioneer women. During the winter, each woman worked on piecing quilt blocks, then sewing them together in strips. She then sewed the strips together to make the quilt top. The bottom of the quilt was made out of a large piece of fabric, sometimes a sheet. Cotton batting was layered between the top and the bottom, or backing. Sometimes people made their own batting in places where cotton was grown. Then they had to carefully pick out all the seeds.

→ PIONEER REMEDIES ←

The mother of a pioneer family was also the family doctor. Often the family lived many miles from a real doctor. So it was up to the mother to nurse her family through all its illnesses and injuries. Pioneer women used a number of home remedies for common problems.

A woman usually had a garden where she raised the herbs she used for her home remedies. She also used many kinds of roots, barks, and other plants to cure illnesses. Dogwood, cherry, and poplar bark in whiskey were used to treat fever. Oil from bee balm was used to treat fungus, bacteria, and parasites. Catnip tea was believed to cure everything from colds to cancer.

The pioneers also made a salve to cure cancer. They boiled several kinds of flowers in vinegar for 24 hours, then added honey and salt. The mixture was supposed to be applied with a feather.

For painful rashes, they used water in which pokeweed had been boiled. The inner bark of the live oak tree was used to cure diarrhea. They rubbed boiled skunk fat on the chest of a person with a sore throat or a cold.

Bloodletting, or bleeding, was thought to cure many conditions. People thought if you had too much blood, your body was out of balance. As a cure, doctors and others "bled" their patients to remove what they thought was excess blood. They did this by either cutting them or applying leeches, worms that suck blood.

Some of the old remedies sound funny to us today. If you had a sore throat, you could cure it by wrapping a dirty sock, still warm from the foot, around your throat. If you had an earache, you needed to get someone to blow smoke into your ear. And if you had a nosebleed, just get someone to drop a cold door key down your back! If a dog bit you, you should take some of his hairs and put them on the wound.

Some were even stranger. If a child had whooping cough, the father should put the head of the sick child into a hole in the meadow at dusk. If you had dandruff, you should wet your hair with kerosene. Apparently most of these remedies didn't work very well. Otherwise, we would still be using them today.

Some people used a worn-out blanket between the layers of the quilt instead of batting. Even worn-out quilts or rags could be used.

The three layers of the quilt were then *basted* together, which means they were sewn with large stitches that would later be removed. The quilt was then placed on a quilting frame. This frame was made from four strips of wood and had legs to raise it to the right height. The women would sit around the frame and quilt the layers together with tiny stitches. The stitches often made designs. Quilting kept the layers of the quilt together so they didn't slip.

Quilting bees were held in homes where there was room for a quilting frame or two to be set up. Sometimes they took down the beds to make room. On a nice day, they sometimes worked outdoors. They might also meet in a school, a church, or a hall with a big room. Quilting bees were a wonderful chance for pioneer women to enjoy the company of other women. They shared family news, child-rearing tips, and news from back home. They also exchanged recipes and quilt patterns. Often they quilted all day, and then in late afternoon, the husbands and boyfriends would arrive for dinner. A dance would sometimes be held in the evening.

Many women kept journals or diaries that told about their lives on the frontier. Some of the letters they wrote have also been saved. Some men kept journals, too. It's interesting to read these and see how life has changed, especially for women.

AN OLD-FASHIONED TAFFY PULL

When pioneer families got together with neighbors, they often enjoyed a taffy pull.
Here's a recipe and directions on how to enjoy this old-fashioned pastime. You need help from an adult to cook the taffy.

What You Need

2 cups sugar
¾ cup water
1¼ cups corn syrup (like Karo Syrup)
1 teaspoon salt
Measuring cups
Measuring spoons
A large pan with heavy bottom and
   straight sides
Big wooden or plastic spoon
Candy thermometer
2 tablespoons butter
1½ teaspoons vanilla
A large platter, greased with butter
Sharp knife
Waxed paper

▸▸◂ ▸◂◂

Measure out the sugar, water, corn syrup, and salt into a pan and turn the burner to low heat. Stir the mixture until the sugar has completely dissolved.

Turn up the heat and put a candy thermometer in the pan, with the tip in the mixture. Let the mixture boil until it reaches 255° F.

Add the butter and vanilla and stir in gently. Pour the mixture on the buttered platter. **WARNING:** It will be very hot!

Wait till the mixture is cool enough to handle. Then, rub butter on your hands. Grab a chunk of taffy in both hands, pull from the center, then fold it back together and pull from the center again. Do this over and over until the taffy turns from a golden color to white.

Stretch taffy into a "rope" and lay on the platter. With the knife, cut the candy into one-inch pieces. Wrap each piece of candy in a piece of waxed paper, twisting the ends. Store uneaten taffy in plastic bags or airtight storage containers.

7
Pioneer Children

A child's life on the 19th-century frontier was very different from the life of a child today. Children had to work a lot harder in those days, because a family couldn't survive if the children didn't do a large part of the work. In the 1800s children were thought of more as small adults, with more responsibilities and less free time than children today.

Off to the West

Pioneer children had different feelings about moving west. Some were excited and thought it was a great adventure. Others didn't want their lives to change. They didn't want to leave friends and relatives behind.

> Altho I was but a girl of 11 years, I distinctly remember many things connected with that far-off time when all of our western country was a wilderness. . . . I remember relations coming to help sew, of tearful partings, little gifts of remembrances exchanged, the sale of the farm, the buying and breaking in of unruly oxen, the loud voices of the men, and the general confusion.
>
> —*Etty Scott, age 11 in 1852*

Children were sorry to leave their friends and schoolmates. They picked up on their parents' feelings about leaving, as well.

This Nebraska family has several children.
Library of Congress LC-DIG-ppmsca-08381

> Never can I forget the morning when we bade farewell. . . . We were surrounded by loved ones, and there stood all my little schoolmates, who had come to kiss me good-bye. My father with tears in his eyes tried to smile as one after another grasped his hands in last farewell. Mama was overcome with grief.
>
> —*Virginia Reed, age 13 in 1846*

The trip was long and hard. If a family moved to Oregon, they were on the move for five or six months. Children who kept journals or diaries wrote about the hardships on the trail. Sarah Sprenger, who was 10 when her family went west, wrote about crossing the Missouri River.

> When we reached the middle of the river, the oxen ran to one side and the boat began to fill with water, until just a tiny bit of the wagon cover was above the water. The oxen swam off; the boatman held my baby brother above the water, Father held Mother up on a wheel of the wagon, while my sister Abbie and brother Jacob kept Nicholas and me from drowning by holding on to us and to the wagon. My oldest sister held to the wagon on a wheel. My brothers Isaac and Charles, one on each side of the river were crazy to come to us, but that was impossible as the river was too full of sand and eddies to swim in . . . my brothers had to run a mile to get a boat. Archie Rusk, a friend of ours who was going with us to Oregon, jumped off the boat to try to get help, though I pleaded with him not to. He was drowned.
>
> —*Sarah Sprenger, age 10 in 1852*

Some children had a better trip. They wrote about their feelings about the trail and what life was like in a wagon train.

When we camp at night, we form a corral with our wagons and pitch our tents on the outside and inside of this corral we drive our cattle, with guards stationed on the outside of tents. We have a cooking stove made of sheet iron, a portable table, tin plates and cups, cheap knives and forks, camp stools, etc. . . . We live on bacon, ham, rice, dried fruits, molasses, packed butter, bread, coffee, tea, and milk as we have our own cows.

—Sallie Hester, age 14 in 1849

Children had chores to do on the trail. In one family, the Scotts, the father assigned the older children duties before they left home. Eighteen-year-old Fanny, the oldest girl, was to do the cooking. Jennie, 17, had the job of keeping a journal of the trip. Meg, 15, helped with the cooking and the journal. Catherine, 13, was called Kit. Her job was to care for the two youngest children, Maria, 5, and Willie, 4. Etty, 11, was to ride the old mare and drive the loose stock. Henry, 9, helped drive his mother's wagon. When Willie died on the Oregon Trail, Kit was left with only Maria to care for.

A boy and his mother drive oxen on the trail.
Library of Congress LC-DIG-ppmsca-02506

Mother kept the two youngest with her always in "Mother's wagon." . . . My brother Willie fell sick. It was in the heat of August. The train was halted, that the darling child of 4 years could be better cared for, but he became unconscious and passed away.

—Etty Scott, age 11 in 1846

Older children did lots of other work on the trail, too. They herded the animals and milked the cows. Sometimes they drove the oxen that pulled the wagons. They also fetched water and gathered firewood and buffalo chips to burn.

Most children didn't get any formal schooling on the trip west, but they still learned a lot and had many interesting experiences. They practiced reading from the Bible, and many kept journals. Along the way, they saw animals like buffalo and landmarks like Chimney Rock and Devils Tower.

They also had the chance to meet Native Americans. Most wagon trains traded with Indi-

(above) **Men and boys had a lot of wood to chop.**
Library of Congress LC-USZ62-68312

(right) **A child helps her mother churn butter.**
Library of Congress LC-USZ62-56652

ans along the trail. Many kids were scared of the Indians and thought they might be kidnapped. Usually, though, the Indians they met were friendly.

Children did find time to play along the trail, though. At night there were campfires, with singing and dancing. They played the same games that they had played at home. They also enjoyed picking flowers and playing with animals, as kids do now. It was fun playing with the new friends they had made and exploring the area where they were.

Eliza Donner was only three when her family went west, but in later years she would remember her time on the trail:

> We little folk sat in the wagons with our dolls, watching the huge white-covered "prairie schooners." During a rest break, we children, who had been confined to the wagons so many hours each day, stretched our limbs, and scampered off in Mayday frolics. We waded the creek, made mud pies, and gathered posies.
>
> —*Eliza Donner, age 3 in 1846*

Settling Down

Once they reached their new homes, life settled down some for the pioneer children. It was still a difficult life, since they were building homes. Also, the homes were not like the ones they had left behind. Most had fairly nice homes back east, with carpet, curtains, and nice furniture. Their first homes in the West were rougher.

Many of the pioneers were homesteaders. With a farm to run, the parents needed all the help the children could give. The mothers also needed help in the house with the cooking, cleaning, sewing, and other work.

The older boys chopped wood to keep the fire going in the fireplace. They also helped to clear the land and build the house. Sometimes the boys went hunting with their father. Boys and sometimes girls worked in the fields raising crops. Boys fished, raked ashes out of the fireplace, and milked the cows.

Girls were more likely to help their mothers with the garden. They planted seeds, weeded the garden, and picked the vegetables when they were ready. Girls also helped with the cooking. They often cared for the younger children. They also helped to care for the sick.

Pioneer girls learned to sew. Most four-year-old girls had learned to sew an apron. Almost every pioneer girl made a sampler. It showed all the fancy stitches they had learned and usually included their name and the date.

Girls helped make new clothes and mend the old ones. If the mother had a spinning wheel, the girls learned to spin wool into yarn. Besides making and mending clothes, girls helped to wash them on laundry day. By the time a girl grew up, she could do all the chores necessary to run a house.

Both boys and girls carried water, collected eggs, and fed chickens and other animals. Even younger children could find kindling and bring the wood into the house. They also picked berries and helped dip candles and make soap.

If the family lived in town and the father was a tradesman, the boys were usually trained to follow the same trade—they helped their fathers in the shop. Storekeepers' children waited on customers, dusted the shelves, and helped to put the merchandise on the shelves.

Getting Dressed

Pioneer children wore different types of clothing than they had back east. The young girls were used to pretty dresses at home.

Our clothing was made suitable for traveling, dresses of plaid linsy, aprons of Scotch gingham, high in the neck, with long sleeves, belt waists and little collars. No more use for low necked short sleeved, pretty little white dresses, with blue and pink sashes, and cute little slippers. All those things were givin away. I remember when I first dressed up in my uniform for the planes, as we called it, How strangely I felt. The very clothing seemed to indicate that we were expected to endure something.

—*Virginia Reed, age 13 in 1846*

For some children, their dress was completely different from that they had worn at home.

Most of us wore for convenience the costume called Bloomers and did not have many changes.

—*Emeline Trimble, age 13 in 1860*

Pioneer children helped pick berries.
Library of Congress LC-DIG-nclc-05328

Pioneers still didn't have many changes of clothes after they were settled. Most girls had two dresses for work and play and one Sunday dress. Their dresses were usually made from cotton. They were a bit shorter than those back home, because of the dirt and mud. Girls wore aprons over their dresses to keep from getting the dresses dirty. Aprons were easier to wash. Girls wore bonnets when they went outside to keep the sun and wind off their faces and necks. Most girls hated the sunbonnets.

Those sunbonnets, with which my head was sheathed every time I started out into the airy out-of-doors, were my chief pests. I usually compromised my integrity by untying the strings as soon as I was out of sight.

—Sarah Bixby Smith, age 6 in 1877

Sarah Smith said she doubled back the corners of the bonnet to make it into a "sort of cocked hat" and tied the strings in a bow on top, letting her "poor scratched ears out of captivity."

In winter, children kept warm by dressing in layers. They wore thick stockings, wool mittens, mufflers, and wool wristlets. *Wristlets* were knitted bands worn to keep the area above the mittens warm.

Mama dressed us in long-legged heavy underwear, long black stockings, overshoes, several slips, bloomers, and warm dresses, coats, bonnets, scarves, and leather mittens. We had long, shining, blonde braids tied with ribbons, and she kept us very clean.

—Sylvia Dye, age and date unknown

Pioneer boys wore dresses until they were about five years old, when they began to wear pants. Until they were about 13, they wore woolen or cotton knickers. They came just below the knee and were held up by suspenders. They seldom had pockets. Young Jesse Applegate said it was because "the strain on the suspenders would be come too great" because of all the "treasures" boys would put in their pockets. Getting long pants was a symbol of manhood for a pioneer boy. Boys also wore hand-made shirts.

Most shoes on the frontier were made by the families, although sometimes they were made by a cobbler or shoemaker.

> [My father] bought a side of upper leather and one of sole leather and had a shoe maker come to the house with his [bench] and tools and shoe the family.
>
> —*Keturah Penton, age unknown in 1836*

There were no right or left shoes. At night, children set out the shoes in the order they had worn them. After wearing them for awhile, they gradually conformed to the shapes of the child's feet and were more comfortable.

School Time

School was a big part of many pioneer children's lives. In the Northwest Territory, where many families settled, the Northwest Ordinance of 1787 stated that a square mile of land must be set aside in each township for a school.

At first, students were taught by a part-time teacher who was paid by the parents and boarded at the homes of the students. Often school was only in session from after the fall harvest until it was time to plant in the spring. And even if school was open in the fall and spring, the older boys stayed home to help on the farm. In some areas, girls were not allowed to attend school. It was believed that they should stay at home and help their mothers with the work in the house.

The teacher might be a young man studying to be a minister or a lawyer. Sometimes the teacher was a young woman, hardly older than the older students. Women often taught only a few years, and then they married. Married women were not allowed to teach.

People did not learn to be teachers by attending college, as they do now. In some places, they only needed an eighth-grade education. In other places, they were required to pass a test. Later special schools, called *normal schools*, were started to train teachers.

Many communities wanted women to teach because they only had to pay them about 60 percent as much as they had to pay a male teacher. In the 1880s, the average female teacher received $54.50 a year, while a male teacher made $71.40 a year. Many women went to teach in the West. Some were looking for a husband, and there were more unmarried men than women on the frontier.

The pioneer school was usually a one-room log building, heated by a stove which burned wood or coal.

(left) **An old-time schoolmaster sharpens his quill pen while a child waits.**
Library of Congress LC-USZ62-69057

(below) **Stoves were used in pioneer schoolhouses.**
Photo by author, courtesy Garst Museum, Greenville, Ohio

➛ TEACHERS' RULES ➛

Pioneer teachers often had to follow strict guidelines. The following list of rules was used by various school districts in Kansas in the second half of the 1800s.

FEMALE TEACHERS OF THIS DISTRICT SHALL NOT:

- Marry or engage in other unseemly conduct during their contract.

- Keep company with men.

- Be away from their domicile [home] between the hours of 8 p.m. and 6 a.m. unless attending a school function.

- Loiter in town ice cream stores.

- Dye their hair.

- Wear face powder, mascara, or lip paint.

- Wear bright colored dresses more than two inches above the ankle.

MALE TEACHERS OF THIS DISTRICT SHALL NOT:

- Frequent pool halls, public halls, saloons, or taverns.

- Get shaved in a barber shop.

- Take more than one evening per week for courting (unless attending church regularly—in which case two evenings may be used).

Failure to abide by these rules will give reason to suspect one's worth, intention, honesty, and integrity. Faithful performances will result in an increase of 25 cents per period providing the board of trustees approves.

[It was] a little log cabin located along the Yellowstone River. The cabin was owned by my father, O. N. Newman. It was low and small (maybe ten by twelve feet, with a window at each end of the structure). I don't think it would have held more than 12 seats, the teacher's desk, and one bench up front where we went to recite our lessons.

—*Sarah Newman, about her first school, age and date unknown*

Pioneer students often sat on split-log benches. The flat side was the seat, and legs were attached to the rounded part of the log. Usually these seats had no backs. Later some of the schools had long desks placed in front of the benches. That made it easier for students to write.

At first students did all their work on slates, which were small blackboards they held in their hands. Later, when it was easier to get paper, they wrote some of their lessons on paper with a *quill pen*. A quill pen was made from a feather on which the *quill*, or pointed end, was split so that

An old school slate.

Photo by author, courtesy Garst Museum, Greenville, Ohio

it would hold ink. Students dipped their pens into bottles of ink, wrote a few words, and then dipped again. The desks had *inkwells*, which were small, round holes that held an ink bottle.

If girls attended school, they sat on one side of the room while boys sat on the other. Sometimes the teacher punished children by making a girl sit on the boy's side or a boy sit on the girl's side. If children didn't know their lessons, they sometimes had to stand with their noses against the wall for a long period of time, or they might have to sit on the "dunce stool" and wear a pointed dunce cap.

Most punishment was more severe than that, though. Teachers always had long, heavy rulers. If children disobeyed orders or talked without permission, they were beaten on the palm of the hand with a ruler. They sometimes were whipped for misbehaving or not knowing lessons. Teachers believed children would learn better if they were afraid of being punished.

Where whippings were common, there were a certain number of lashes for each "crime." The whip could cut through clothing and skin. At one school, you got 8 lashes for swearing, 10 lashes for "misbehaving to girls," 4 lashes for boys and girls playing together, and 8 lashes for telling lies.

All ages of children were taught in the same room. The small children sat near the front and the bigger ones in the back. Often the teacher would call one grade to the front of the room to recite their lesson.

The smallest children worked on learning their ABCs. The children who were a little older learned to read and spell, and to do arithmetic problems. The teacher also taught history. Most

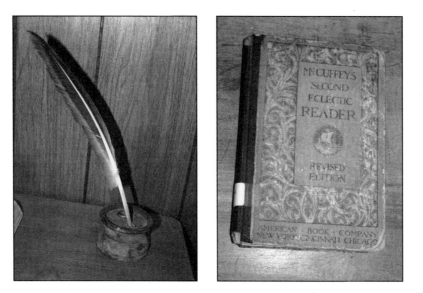

(left) **A quill pen and ink bottle used in an old school.**
Photo by author, courtesy Garst Museum, Greenville, Ohio

(right) **Pioneer children learned to read from McGuffey readers.**
Photo by author, courtesy Garst Museum, Greenville, Ohio

teachers taught by having the children memorize facts and recite them back.

Penmanship, or handwriting, was very important. The children sometimes had copy books, made from a few pages of paper bound together. The teacher would write a sentence at the top of the page, and then the student would try to copy it as neatly as the teacher had written it.

Textbooks, if they had them, were not the brightly illustrated books students have today. There were few pictures, and those that were included were black-and-white line drawings. Sometimes children learned to read from a book brought from home. Often it was the Bible, which was oftentimes the only book a family owned. Sometimes children were lucky enough to have a McGuffey Reader or Speller.

Pioneer children did have recess. In some schools, the boys and girls were separated on the playground. In other schools, they were allowed to play together. They played games like Tag,

→ STUDENT ← RULES, 1860

Boys and girls shall file into class-room in separate lines and be seated quietly on opposite sides of the room.

Boys shall remove their caps when entering.

Children must sit up straight at all times.

Children must not squirm, fidget or whine.

Children must be clean and tidy in clothing.

There will be a daily inspection of neck, ears, and fingernails prior to class to ensure cleanliness of person.

Young ladies must never show a bare ankle; girls' and boys' clothing should cover arms and legs completely.

Blindman's Bluff, and Duck, Duck, Goose. When recess was over, the teacher came to the door and rang a big bell to call the students back to class.

Most schools had two outhouses or outdoor toilets, one for the boys and one for the girls. However, one school in Washington State didn't have any. The teacher complained about the lack of a toilet.

> When I told the directors that I could not teach if they did not build one, one of them remarked to the others, "Now you see what comes of hiring someone from the Outside. We never had any trouble before, and there are plenty of trees to get behind."
>
> —*A Washington teacher, c. 1863*

Schools were sometimes the only public buildings in an area, so they were often the center of social life. Community-wide spelling bees were often held at the schools. They also had singing classes, where someone taught songs to the children and adults. In later years, debates and traveling lectures were often held in school buildings.

Play Time

Pioneer children spent a lot of time working and going to school. But they did have some time for play. They had a few toys, too, and many were homemade. Sometimes their parents made the toys, and sometimes the children made them themselves.

William Wright had a hand-carved wooden flute that he loved to play. One morning, it was missing.

(left) **Teachers rang bells when recess was over.**
Photo by author, courtesy Garst Museum, Greenville, Ohio

(below) **Boys play a game of Crack the Whip during recess.**
Library of Congress LC-USZ62-25016

> I searched everywhere for the flute, but I couldn't find it. When my brother, John, suggested that someone might have thrown it in the morning cooking fire, I cried. I pled with my father to make another one for me, but he could never manage to find the time.
>
> —*William Wright, age unknown in 1846*

Many toys were made of wood. Some fathers carved wooden animals for their children. Boys liked to whittle things out of wood with a pocket knife. Children had wooden tops to spin, and some had marbles. They also played games with string, such as Cat's Cradle. Rolling hoops was a favorite pastime. The hoop was a large wooden

BLINDMAN'S BLUFF

Blindman's Bluff was often played by groups of pioneer children. It could be played outdoors in good weather. Try playing it with a group of your friends.

What You Need

Scarf or piece of cloth for a blindfold
Area large enough for several people to move around

◄●► ◄●►

Find a large, safe area with nothing to trip over or run into. Choose one person to be It and tie a blindfold over that person's eyes so he or she cannot see.

Twirl the person who is It around several times. The other players scatter, and It tries to tag one of them. The player who is tagged is the next one to be It.

In some versions of the game, the players make noises to give It a better chance. In other versions, the player who is It has to guess who he or she has caught.

LETTER TO A FRIEND BACK HOME

Pretend you're a pioneer child. You've been in your new home for several months now. Write a letter back home to your best friend. Tell him or her all about your life in the West. Remember to tell your friend about your house, the weather, the school you attend, and what you do for fun.

◄●► ◄●►

CLOTHESPIN DOLL

Some little girls made dolls from clothespins. You can do the same thing today.

What You Need

Clothespin, the kind with a round top (not a clip)
Fine tip pens or markers
Pipe cleaner
Scraps of yarn
Scissors
Glue
Scraps of cloth or felt

Use markers or pens to draw eyes, nose, and mouth for a face on the round, top part of a clothespin.

Wrap the center of a pipe cleaner around the doll's neck and bend its two ends to make arms. Bend a small loop in each end to form hands.

Cut yarn pieces twice as long as you want the hair to be. Glue the strands across the top of the clothespin so they hang down the sides. Braid each side of the hair or make ponytails by tying with a different color yarn. If it's a boy doll, make his hair shorter.

Use scraps of cloth and felt to make clothes for the doll. Glue the pieces to the doll as you go. Use the marker to draw shoes on the bottoms of both legs.

Have fun with your doll. You might want to make a whole family!

one, often off a barrel. The child ran along behind the hoop, pushing it with a stick. Sometimes they had races or tried to see who could keep his hoop rolling the longest.

Most girls had some sort of doll. It might be a rag doll, like Elizabeth Conner's:

> She wasn't much to look at, just a few rags loosely stitched together, but she was real to me. I talked to her, and sometimes it seemed to me that she talked to me. We laughed together. We cried together. We made the trek [west] together. She was my playmate, my best friend, and I was happier because she was there.
>
> —*Elizabeth Conner, about her doll, Lizzie, age and date unknown*

Dolls were made of whatever materials were available. Some dolls were made from cornhusks or corncobs. Others fashioned dolls from clothespins. They were dressed with clothing made from scraps of material.

Girls sometimes had other toys, too. Some had toy dishes sent by relatives in the East. Occasionally they would be lucky enough to have a book or two.

Both boys and girls played with balls and wooden stilts. Many children enjoyed a wooden toy called a Whimmydiddle, a notched stick with a rotor, or propeller, on the end. You held the Whimmydiddle in your left hand and rubbed another stick up and down across the notches. This made the rotor turn. Children also played with a homemade toy sometimes known as a Moonwinder or Buzz Saw.

Children played many games, too. To play Duck, Duck, Goose, the children sat in a circle. One person was It and went around the circle, tapping each child on the head and saying, "Duck." When he tapped someone and said, "Goose," that person had to jump up and chase It, who tried to get back around to the Goose's place in the circle without being tapped.

Pioneer children also played Leapfrog. Players stood in a line, and the last person jumped or leaped over each person in front of him. When he got to the front of the line he crouched down and the new last person in line repeated his actions.

There were seasonal activities, too. In winter children went sledding or ice skating. In spring, children sometimes made kites and flew them. And in the summer, they enjoyed swimming, wading, and gathering flowers.

Children were very creative in their play. One family of children in Nebraska turned muskmelon rinds upside down, tied them to their feet, and skated around the floor of their cabin. Like today's children, they used their imaginations to play "make believe."

Boys playing Leapfrog.
Library of Congress LC-USZ62-61809

(left) **A little boy posing with his hoop in 1885.**
Author's collection

(right) **Little dolls in boxes like this were also popular in pioneer times. A child's grandmother might have sent her one from back east.**
Photo by author, courtesy Garst Museum, Greenville, Ohio

MOONWINDER

This toy was often made from a round disk of wood, about two inches in diameter. But you can make one that works just as well by using a button.

What You Need

Large, flat button
String or yarn, about a yard long

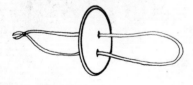

If you want your Moonwinder to be different on both sides, glue two buttons with the flat sides together, but make sure the holes match up.

Thread one end of a piece of string through each of the two holes in the button. (If it has four holes, just use two that are opposite each other). Tie the loose ends of the string together.

Put a forefinger through each loop. Make sure the button is halfway between your fingers.

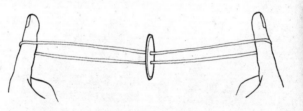

Whirl the button around away from you until the string is wound tight. Then, pull back and forth on the loops. As you move your fingers in and out, the button will spin, making a whirring sound.

8

The End of the Pioneer Era

Many things worked together to bring about the end of the American frontier. It was officially closed by the U.S. Census Bureau in 1890. Every census since the first one in 1790 had contained a map showing where the frontier was. In 1790, that line went through the middle of the Maine coast, the middle of New York State and through Virginia, down to Georgia. The land west of that line was a wild, uncharted, unsettled area. Most of it didn't belong to the colonies.

Thomas Jefferson thought it would take over 2,000 years for the frontier to fill up. But only 80 years later, the U.S. stretched from coast to coast, and the frontier was gone.

Up to and including 1889 the country had a frontier of settlement, but at present the unsettled area has been so broken into by isolated bodies of settlement that there can hardly be said to be a frontier line . . . its westward movement, etc., cannot, therefore, any longer have a place in the census reports.

—*1890 U.S. Census*

Many people felt uneasy about the closing of the frontier. There had always been a frontier—there had always been land available to the west, usually either cheap or free. The West was seen as a land of opportunity. People had always been able to go west to start over. New immigrants often went west. Freed slaves did the same.

Native Americans performing the Ghost Dance.
Library of Congress
LC-USZ62-52423

The Wounded Knee Massacre

There had been friction between Native Americans and settlers throughout the 80 years the frontier was being settled. But the Wounded Knee Massacre ended the wars between the Indians and the settlers.

Around 1890, many Indians were becoming members of a religious movement called the Ghost Dance. Sitting Bull, a leader of the Lakota tribe, asked Kicking Bear to go to the Standing Rock Reservation and preach about the new religion.

My brothers, I bring you the promise of a day in which there will be no white man to lay his hand on the bridle of the Indian horse; when the red men of the prairie will rule the world and not be turned away from the hunting grounds by any man. I bring you word from your fathers, the Ghosts . . .

—*Kicking Bear, 1890*

The Ghost Dance religion was started by Wovoka, a Piute Indian. Kicking Bear quoted him.

The earth is getting old, and I will make it new for my chosen people, the Indians, who are to inhabit it, and among them will be all those of their ancestors who have died. . . . I will cover the earth with new soil to a depth of five times the height of a man, and under this new soil will be buried the whites. . . . The new lands will be covered with sweet-grass and running water and trees, and herds of buffalos and ponies will stray over it, that my red children may eat and drink, hunt and rejoice.

—*Wovoka, 1890*

The U.S. government feared the Ghost Dance was really a war dance and that the Indians were getting ready to go to war. On December 15, 1890, the government sent agents to arrest Sitting Bull at the Standing Rock Reservation. The agents murdered him and eight of his warriors, claiming that he had resisted arrest.

The Lakota turned to Big Foot, a peaceful leader. He and over 350 of his people decided to go to the Pine Ridge Agency, where they thought they would be protected. It was the eighth largest Indian reservation in the United States. Chief Red Cloud at Pine Ridge had promised them food, shelter, and horses. He was also a peaceful leader.

The Lakota made their way through the rugged terrain of the Badlands of South Dakota toward Pine Ridge. It was a dangerous 150-mile walk through freezing winter weather. Chief Big Foot was old and ill with pneumonia.

On December 28, the group was surrounded by the U.S. Cavalry. Big Foot's followers raised a white flag, the sign of peace. The army forced them to go to the bank of Wounded Knee Creek, where four huge cannons pointed down at them. They were made to camp there that night.

Colonel James Forsyth arrived that evening with more troops. He took over as commander. The soldiers questioned the Indians all night, not allowing them to sleep. The Indians were told to surrender their weapons, and most of them threw them in a pile. It was rumored in the Indian camp that the Lakota would be sent to Indian Territory in Oklahoma, where living conditions were terrible.

The next morning, the Indians were asked again for their weapons. A couple of them had guns hidden under their blankets. The rifle of one of the Indians went off, possibly as a soldier tried to take it away from him.

Immediately the soldiers began firing on the Indians. There was no way the unarmed Indians could fight off nearly 500 armed U.S. soldiers. Most of the deaths occurred in the first 20 minutes. Some Lakota tried to escape to a nearby ravine. Soldiers followed them and gunned them down, shouting, "Remember Little Bighorn!" Indian survivors believed this attack was in revenge for Custer's death at the Battle of Little Bighorn 14 years before.

The dead and injured Indians covered the riverbank. A blizzard swept through that night,

Chief Red Cloud
Library of Congress LC-USZ62-91032

The beginning of the Wounded Knee Massacre.
Library of Congress LC-USZ62-89867

killing many of the injured as they lay there, unprotected. About 300 of the Lakota died that night. Many were women and children. When the survivors returned to bury the dead, several babies were found alive, wrapped in the shawls of their dead mothers.

> I can see that something else died there in the bloody mud and was buried in the blizzard. A people's dream died there. It was a beautiful dream . . .
>
> —*Black Elk, a survivor of the massacre, remembering in 1932*

The army called the event the Battle of Wounded Knee, but the Indians resented that name. They believed the event was a massacre rather than a battle. Native tribes had not come to the area to fight, and the soldiers had disarmed them before attacking.

Alaskan homestead
Library of Congress LC-DIG-ppmsc-02166

The massacre marked the end of hostilities between the Indians and the settlers, and removed the last barrier to settling the West. Because of that, this incident also helped to bring the frontier age to an end.

In 1893, a young historian named Frederick Jackson Turner spoke at the Chicago World's Fair. He claimed that the American frontier no longer existed. He said that all the land had been settled. Turner believed that frontier life had given rise to the character of the American hero. He thought pioneers were forced to take care of themselves and their families, and that made them strong people. He believed that until the Westward Movement began, Americans were pretty much like Europeans. He thought that the pioneer era had made the United States into a unique society.

Homesteading did not suddenly end in 1890, just because the U.S. Census said the frontier was closed. It was true that most of the best land was gone by that time. But most of the best land had been bought before the Homestead Act was even passed. Before 1890 ended, 372,659 homesteaders had fulfilled all the conditions to take title to the land they had claimed. More than four times that many have homesteaded in the West since 1890. Many of these homesteads were claimed after 1900.

Last of the Homesteaders

Homesteading was officially ended in most of the country in 1976. The Federal Land Policy and Management Act said only those in Alaska would be allowed to continue homesteading. Homesteading ended there in 1986. So Alaska was actually the last frontier in the United States.

Modern homesteaders in Alaska had a few advantages over those who had homesteaded on the plains or in the far West. It was easier for them to get to their claims. They were able to fly in building materials, electric generators, and other things the earlier pioneers didn't have. They traveled by snowmobile or float plane instead of covered wagons. But the Alaskan climate presented its own challenges to the homesteaders there.

In 2001, Kenneth Deardorff, who lived on the Stony River in southwestern Alaska, was named America's last official homesteader. Deardorff was a Vietnam veteran from California who filed his claim in 1974.

Deardorff and his family lived on the land. They built a house and other buildings, hunted moose and other game for food, and fished for salmon. They faced difficulties, including isolation, wildlife, bad weather, fire, and difficulties with farming.

Although he had fulfilled all the requirements for homesteading by 1979, he didn't actually receive deed to his land until May 1988, making him the last person to receive title to land under the Homestead Act.

Now Deardorff lives in McGrath, a small Alaskan town. He works there as a construction consultant. He sold the cabin in 1993.

So, homesteading has ended in the country—the pioneer era is officially over. Although many were disappointed when they moved west, others made good lives for themselves. They became solid citizens, and their accomplishments and those of their children and grandchildren have contributed much to our country.

❧ Resources ❧

Web Sites to Explore

All About Laura Ingalls Wilder
www.factmonster.com/ipka/A0801303.html
Includes a list of books written by Laura Ingalls Wilder, a list of books written about her, and a time line of her life.

Frontier House: Frontier Life
www.pbs.org/wnet/frontierhouse/frontierlife/index.html
This site for the public TV reality series *Frontier House* contains lots of information on how people lived on the frontier.

The Journals of the Lewis and Clark Expedition
http://lewisandclarkjournals.unl.edu
Here you can read the actual and complete journals written during the expedition by Meriwether Lewis, William Clark, and others who accompanied them.

Just for Kids: Some Pioneer Recipes
www.backwoodshome.com/articles/shober30.html
Features a number of pioneer recipes, plus a word-search puzzle that you can print out and solve.

Life as a Pioneer
www.campsilos.org/mod2/students/life.shtml
This site for kids includes activities such as an Internet scavenger hunt, and links to other pioneer sites.

The Oregon Trail: Crossing the Great Plains by Ox-Wagons
www.isu.edu/~trinmich/00.ar.palmer.html
The memoirs of Harriet Palmer, who crossed the Great Plains in a covered wagon when she was 11 years old.

Oregon Trail 101
www.oregonpioneers.com/OregonHistory_101.htm
All about the Oregon Trail: includes maps, photos, and quotes from many of those who took this trail west.

Pioneer Children: Toys and Games
www.saskschools.ca/~gregory/fun.html
Explores the games and toys pioneer children played with, including directions for making many games.

Pioneer Life
www.42explore2.com/pioneer.htm
Contains links to many other interesting sites about the pioneers.

Pioneers
http://library.thinkquest.org/6400/default.htm
Answers many of the questions you may want to ask about pioneers and their lives.

Books to Read

FICTION

Bunting, Eve. *Dandelions*. San Diego: Harcourt Brace, 1995.*

Harvey, Brett. *Cassie's Journey: Going West in the 1860s*. New York: Holiday, 1988.*

Moss, Marissa. *Rachel's Journey: The Story of a Pioneer Girl*. San Diego: Harcourt Brace, 1998.*

Wilder, Laura Ingalls. The *Little House* books. New York: Harper-Collins.*

NONFICTION

Carlson, Laurie. *Westward Ho!: An Activity Guide to the Wild West*. Chicago: Chicago Review Press, 1996.*

Davis, Kenneth C. *Don't Know Much About Pioneers*. New York: HarperCollins, 2003.*

Dickinson, Rachel. *Great Pioneer Projects You Can Build Yourself*. White River Junction, VT: Nomad Press, 2007.*

Duncan, Dayton. *Lewis & Clark: The Journey of the Corps of Discovery*. New York: A.A. Knopf, 1997.

Freedman, Russell. *Children of the Wild West*. New York: Clarion, 1983.*

Giff, Patricia Reilly. *Laura Ingalls Wilder: Growing Up in the Little House*. New York: Viking Kestrel, 1987.*

Greenwood, Barbara. *Pioneer Crafts*. Toronto: Kids Press, 1995.*

Herndon, Sarah Raymond. *Days on the Road: Crossing the Plains in 1865*. Guilford, CT: Two Dot, 2003.

Holmes, Kenneth, ed. *Covered Wagon Women*. Vol. 1, *Diaries & Letters from the Western Trails, 1840–1849*. Lincoln, NE: Bison Books, 1995.

Kimball, Violet T. *Stories of Young Pioneers: In Their Own Words*. Missoula, MT: Mountain Press, 2000.*

Wadsworth, Ginger. *Words West: Voices of Young Pioneers*. New York: Clarion, 2003.*

Werner, Emmy E. *Pioneer Children on the Journey West*. New York: Basic Books, 1996.

---

* Children's book

❧ Index ❦